HOW TO BE
A REALLY
NICE PERSON

HOW TO BE A REALLY NICE PERSON

DOING THE RIGHT THING— YOUR WAY

PAT COLLINS

WITH JOHN MALONE

M. Evans and Company, Inc.
New York

Library of Congress Cataloging in Publication Data

Collins, Pat.
  How to be a really nice person.

  Includes index.
  1. Conduct of life. I. Malone, John. II. Title
BJ1581.2.C575   1983   395   83-1759

ISBN 0-87131-406-1

M. Evans and Company, Inc.
216 East 49 Street
New York, New York 10017

Design by Diane Gedymin

Manufactured in the United States of America

9 8 7 6 5 4 3 2 1

TO JOE RAPOSO

Contents

Acknowledgments

I want to thank Walter and Betsy Cronkite, John Malone, Joan Witberg, Bill Adler, Leonard Franklin, Irene and Bill Collins, Joan and Bob Tisch, Albert Capraro, Linda Cabasin, Herb Katz, and all the other people who have made it easy for me to be a nice person.

Introduction

When I told my husband, the composer Joe Raposo, that I was planning to write a book about how to be a nice person in today's very complicated world, he laughed and said, "You?" I laughed myself, because I knew just what he was talking about. After all, as a network television critic, I'd panned a lot of movies and Broadway shows over the years, which doesn't do much to convince people of your niceness, even if you happen to be right on target. I'd also interviewed hundreds of celebrities on the air, and the art of interviewing involves asking the kind of challenging questions that some people will inevitably take amiss.

But, in another way, that was exactly the point. Being a nice person isn't a matter of image, it's a way of living. It's a matter of responding to other people in a way that avoids putting them down unnecessarily, but at the same time maintains your own standards and integrity. That's never been an easy tightrope to walk, of course. And it's more difficult than ever in today's world. We've been through Doing Your Own Thing and the Me Decade, and now find ourselves trying to cope with the Age of Total Honesty. It's been drummed into us since the late sixties that if we want to get ahead in our extremely fast-paced, highly competitive society, we'd better learn how to manipulate other people, always look out for number one, and keep a steely eye on the main chance. There's no question that you've got to look out for yourself. But is that really incompatible with being a nice person? Isn't it possible to look out for your own interests *and* take into consideration the needs of other people?

I believe very strongly that it is possible. I believe that most of us want very much to be nice to other people, to be helpful, supportive and, yes, liked. Certainly, we're all curious about whether or not other people are nice. The first question I'm usually asked about the movie stars, recording artists, and best-selling authors I interview is: "Was he nice?" or "Is she a nice person?" The answer is often yes, and sometimes surprising to people. Clint Eastwood, for all his tough-guy image, is one of the most straightforward and decent men in Hollywood. Despite his flamboyant reputation, Burt Reynolds is modest to the point of self-deprecation. Dudley Moore, Goldie Hawn, Gregory Peck and Alan Alda are people you'd want in your lifeboat if the ship went down.

There are exceptions, of course. One very well known television and film actress comes across on the television screen during an interview as warm, open and friendly. But she seems to save all her energy for appearing nice while the camera is on her, and is often very distant with the production staff and technical crew and even the interviewer at other moments. She has been known, moreover, to grab a doughnut out of a crew member's mouth and throw it away. This actress is a great believer in a healthy diet, and apparently thinks that she's doing people a favor—indeed, being a nice person—when she takes away their "junk" food. But it isn't usually a much appreciated gesture.

In fact, one of the major problems in determining how to behave nicely is that niceness tends to lie in the eye of the beholder. It's all too easy to get confused. There are a great many people, for instance, who promise what they can't deliver in an effort to be nice. They say they'll be glad to pick up the theater tickets, or make the restaurant reservations, or meet you at the airport, and then either forget to do it or do it badly. It would really be better for everyone in the long run—and nicer on their part—if they said right up front that they can't do whatever it is.

Other people keep trying to prove how nice they are, but in the process often succeed in making other people feel lousy. They say things like this: "I just talked to Sally in the hospital. She got my flowers and she's feeling much better." This statement, of course, is really a question: Where are your flowers?

Matters are made even more complicated by the fact that the traditional rules that used to help define niceness have been eroded, turned upside down, or in some cases simply discarded. There used to be a commonly understood rule, for example, that if you couldn't give someone a compliment on the way he or she was dressed, you kept your mouth shut. No longer. These days you're just as likely to be told that you really shouldn't be wearing those tacky shoes with that elegant dress. And the people who say that kind of thing actually believe they're being nice. They're friends, and by being honest with you they're showing how much they care. You may wish they cared a little less, because all they've succeeded in doing is hurting you.

A trivial hurt? Perhaps. But if you inflict a trivial hurt, it means that it's an unnecessary hurt. What's more, trivial hurts mount up. We all have thousands of chances every day to be nice or not so nice. In my own life, I interact with dozens of people every day, from secretaries, to camerapersons, to program guests. But that's only part of my life. I am also a wife, the mother of two children, and stepmother to Joe's two sons by a previous marriage. We're a very close family and I also see a great deal of both Joe's parents and my own. That adds up to a lot of people to be nice to. It also adds up to a great many chances to hurt people, however trivially, for no good reason. That is something I don't want to do, and over the years I have worked out a series of guidelines for myself—not rules but guidelines—that I use in my own on-going attempt at being a nice person. They are guidelines I believe can work for anyone.

Nice People Don't

We need new guidelines because the strictly ordered social mores of the past so often don't apply anymore. It used to be that being a nice person simply meant adhering to a well-defined set of rules, including a long list of don'ts. "Nice people don't do that, dear," parents used to admonish.

Nice people don't spit in public.
Nice people don't swear.
Nice people don't talk about sex.
Nice people don't live together unless they're married.
Nice people don't get divorced.

The only don't on that list that still carries any weight is the first. Nice people still don't spit in public, but they do swear, talk about sex constantly, live together without benefit of matrimony, and get divorced in droves.

There was a good deal of hypocrisy involved in all those past don'ts, of course. Your Aunt Agatha's behavior, for instance, may have been the model of correctness, as she observed every don't in the book, but the entire family knew that beneath that proper exterior lay the soul of a harridan. Still, the rules were in place and everyone knew pretty much what was expected of them if they wanted to be looked upon as being nice. A person who exhibited a true generosity of spirit as well as obeying the rules was spoken of as being "really nice," a distinction that recognized the fact that mere correctness, while essential, wasn't the whole story.

These days, unhappily, mere correctness isn't even half the story. I say unhappily because even though what used to be regarded as correct was often based on hypocrisy, chauvinism, or even oppression, we are now faced with a kind of anarchy. It still seems to be generally agreed that it isn't nice to try to steal someone else's husband or wife (or live-in partner, for that matter), especially if you know both halves of the couple. And there are some small matters of simple etiquette that continue to retain a goodly number of adherents, such as the social usefulness of saying please and thank you, and the cosmetic desirability of chewing with one's mouth closed. But "good manners," too, can get you into trouble these days. Some women with strong feminist leanings, for instance, get annoyed when a man holds a door for them, seeing that act not as a natural courtesy but as a come-on or put-down (which it may in fact sometimes be), and therefore not nice.

Etiquette, in and of itself, won't suffice anymore in dealing with the complexities of the 1980s. What's "correct" in one situation, or with one individual, may easily cause irritation or give actual offense in another case. What one person thinks is niceness someone else may regard as being anything but.

Is it nice to tell a good friend that his or her new romantic interest is a boor or a bore? Some people think so, in the name of being honest or saving people from themselves.

Is it nice for a guest at a party to break out several joints of marijuana and offer them around? Some people would think they were being generous.

Is it nice to lecture friends on their eating habits or tell them to stop smoking so much? Many people certainly feel it's their business to make their friends into healthier and supposedly happier people.

Is it nice to give someone who's having serious financial problems an even more lavish birthday present than usual? Many people would feel that the extra expense showed how much they cared.

The difficulty is that all of these situations—and dozens of similar ones—are chockablock with ambiguity. There may be times when it *is* helpful, friendly, and nice to call someone's attention to the deficiencies of a person he or she has become involved with, or to suggest that someone needs to take better care of his or her health. In other cases, such "helpfulness," however well meant, may be an unwarranted intrusion into the person's private life.

If a guest knows that his or her hosts smoke pot, and buy it themselves regardless of the legalities, then offering a joint may be perfectly acceptable behavior—depending on who else is present. But it could also create embarrassment all around.

A lavish gift to someone in financial straits could be the perfect expression of one's concern and caring, or a form of charitable overkill—depending on the precise kind of gift and the nature of the personal relationship.

Our impulses may be helpful, friendly, and nice. But the question is: Are the actions we take on the basis of those "nice" impulses going to appear that way to other people, or may they cause distress? How can we know?

And, perhaps even more important, if someone else's actions do distress us, how can we tell them off nicely? How can we control the situation, and persuade people to behave as we would like them to without stooping to their level or behaving rudely ourselves? How do we react?

We live in a world that has not only changed but is continuing to change at a very rapid rate. We can't act nicely or react nicely in such a world according to set rules. We have to be flexible. But we need some starting points. Since the perspective of any two people may be quite different in respect to the same set of circumstances, we must above all learn to read the contexts we find ourselves in.

Defining the Context

"You really are mean."

Not very nice words.

Or are they? It all depends on the context.

Uttered in anger or as an accusation, they could be very upsetting words. But if, for instance, they were spoken by a wife to her husband when he refuses to tell her where he's taking her for her birthday, they could be loving and humorous words.

Being a nice person means always taking into account the context you find yourself in, and behaving, or reacting, in a way that is appropriate to that context. On the surface, defining the context seems simple enough. It's merely a matter of identifying the who, the what, the where, and the when.

Who are you dealing with?
What are the circumstances?
Where are the events unfolding?
When is the situation occurring?

The problem is, of course, that each of these four factors interacts with the others, modifying the meaning of the situation. Suppose, for example, that the who is the husband of one of your closest friends. Lately he's developed something of a drinking problem. Ordinarily, he's a very sweet guy, but too much liquor sometimes turns him nasty. You know why he's drinking too much. He seems to have come to a dead end in the hierarchy of the firm he works for, stuck at the middle-management level, with younger men being advanced over him. The fact that he's the husband of such a close friend means that you're willing to put up with more from him than would be the case with a lot of other people in the same circumstances. If you weren't so close to the couple, you might simply avoid seeing them. But your friend needs all the support she can get. That's the what of it.

The where and when of the matter affect your feelings about the situation, however. It's one thing if your friend's husband gets drunk when you're at *their* home, but quite another if it's at your house or at a restaurant. In terms of the when, if he's already three sheets to the wind before dinner is even served, it means there's a long and possibly unpleasant evening ahead of you. If it's fairly late when he begins to fall apart, the situation takes on a different cast.

Your feelings are going to vary depending on how all these different factors come together on a given occasion. It's likely to be much easier to be nice about his drinking if the hour is late, and you're at his house, and it's time to leave anyway, than if he arrives at your house already half-plastered at seven in the evening and starts acting aggressively toward your other guests. The context is not only going to affect your attitude, it's also going to require different kinds of responses from you.

In the course of this book I'm going to be discussing dozens of tricky situations in which any one of us is liable to find ourselves in today's world. In each case, I'll be focusing on the context and its meaning. Then, we'll be looking at how the situation can be handled your way.

We're all individuals, with personality quirks, special likes and dislikes, and different perspectives on the world. But there are certain guidelines that are readily adaptable to individual application. Even though there may not be any one "correct" way to deal with a particular situation, the guidelines can be used to help you determine the nicest way you can handle it that is consistent with *your* values and sense of self.

This is not a book of etiquette, nor is it my aim to create an encyclopedia. It is a book about coping with the problems that we all face in dealing nicely with people who, whether inadvertently or on purpose, through ignorance or because of different standards, put us in the position of responding to situations that can lead to hurt feelings and embarrassment on all sides if they're handled in the wrong way. It is a book based on my own experiences—including an all too plentiful sampling of my own past mistakes—which taught me a lesson. Like anybody else, I have put my foot in my mouth because I spoke too quickly or failed to realize exactly who I was talking to and what the circumstances called for; I have imposed on other people when I shouldn't have; said no in ways that were unnecessarily harsh or insensitive; and dealt with changing relationships by taking the coward's way out. Also, like anybody else, I have been treated rudely, put down, and made to feel awful by people who weren't being at all nice; I have been asked to take on unfair responsibilities, imposed upon, asked a lot of questions I didn't want to answer, and been forced to take sides when I would rather have stayed out of it.

In the course of these experiences I have come to believe that the nice person has three main responsibilities. First, there is the responsibility to avoid hurting other people, embarrassing them, or putting them in an untenable position. The nice person's second responsibility is to respond to awkward, difficult, or unpleasant situations in ways that best fulfill the objective of preventing a bad situation from getting worse. Finally, the nice person has a responsibility to himself or herself. The phrase "nice guys finish last" was invented by people who'd sell their grandmothers to get ahead to excuse the fact that they're not nice people. A great many very nice people are just as successful as the walk-all-over-you power-trippers of this world—and almost always happier and more fulfilled as well. In most circumstances, being nice will get you a great deal further in the long run than being the opposite. When we're nice to other people we're doing ourselves a favor. That doesn't mean, of course, that we have to turn the other cheek whatever the provocation. Being a nice person doesn't mean being a doormat; it means *trying* to deal with situations nicely while reserving the right to be responsible to one's own standards and sense of self when niceness doesn't work.

As we explore the meaning of niceness, and the techniques and guidelines I've developed, I'll be looking at situations involving strangers, old friends and new, co-workers, and family members. The forming of new relationships, the ending of old ones, the reordering of existing ones is a merry-go-round of growth and decay and renewal that has always been a part of the human experience. But the merry-go-round spins faster for Americans today than it ever has before; often, it may seem that we're spinning out of control. We change jobs; move from one neighborhood or city to another; marry, divorce, and remarry at an almost manic pace. As a result, many of us end up with too many people in our lives. Trying to compensate for the underlying loneliness that comes from so much moving around, so much change, many of us try to form emotional connections with as many people as we can. But when you have too many people in your life, it is easy to stretch yourself too thin, to lose patience too easily. Then, at the slightest sign of trouble, it's goodbye. After all, as the lyric from Stephen Sondheim's musical *Company* expresses it, "Another hundred people just got off of the train." There's always someone new to try to make a connection with.

But being a nice person—and a happy person—means nurturing the relationships that exist. Patience is crucial to being a nice person, and when there are too many people to be nice to, our patience can become literally exhausted. Some of us can handle more relationships—and more complex relationships—than others, but all of us have our limits.

The nice person, after all, needs to have some strength and patience in reserve. People we care about are going to have problems, at one time or another—we all do. An illness in the family, a sister or brother or close friend who is suddenly in the throes of divorce, a child who has fallen in with the wrong friends, a relative who's going bankrupt, a parent who is in bad health—all of them may abruptly need extra attention and care and niceness from us. I'll be looking at many situations involving people in trouble, people with problems, and examining the issue of when to help, how best to help, and when it is more appropriate to let well enough alone. What is the context of the particular situation? How honest can you or should you be with the person? Might it be that a few white lies are going to be more helpful than complete frankness? How much help, in terms of your own emotional well-being, can you afford to give?

This last is a very important point. "Some people are more nice than wise," wrote the eighteenth-century English poet William Cowper. Those words are as true now as they were two centuries ago. While the object of this book is to show how difficult situations and people can be handled in a nice way, it needs to be emphasized that niceness can be carried too far and that there are times when it's important to draw the line.

Being a nice person doesn't mean allowing oneself to be walked over. For one thing, not even the nicest person can succeed at trying to keep everybody happy all of the time. Choices have to be made, and one should never allow oneself to be forced—or blackmailed—into being nice. People who are "too nice" and not sufficiently wise end up being taken for granted. And once your niceness starts being taken for granted, it begins to lose its meaning and its power to help. There are many cases in which being too nice isn't going to help solve the problem at hand. What's more, being too nice can raise false hopes, and ultimately make a problem worse. There are times when even the really nice person must put his or her foot down, and say, in effect: "You're taking advantage of me. That's enough."

Nice people have rights, too.

Part 1
BEING NICE AND BEING YOU

1

Bringing Back the White Lie

We are living in the Age of Total Honesty. In the name of being honest, up-front, really frank, and fully in touch with oneself, people everywhere are saying perfectly dreadful things to one another and claiming that it's the right thing to do. I flinch every time I hear the phrase, "As a friend, I really have to tell you . . ." I flinch when I overhear someone saying it to someone else, and I immediately steel myself for the worst when it's directed at me. People think they can run down other people's taste, personal habits, friends, lovers, children, and spouses with impunity, all in the guise of being "helpful." Personally, I think total honesty is an affront to five thousand years of civilization. It's self-indulgent, destructive, hurtful, even cruel, and not at all nice.

It is more than time to restore the white lie to its rightful and extremely important place in human affairs.

Civilization was built on white lies. They are the salve that makes it possible for human beings to take even tentative steps toward living together in some approximation of peace and harmony. The nice person, in my view, not only has the right to tell white lies, but the duty to do so. Let's make a distinction. The utter lie—the black lie, if you will— is used to cover up some kind of crime, be it adultery or embezzlement, or to deliberately and falsely sully someone else's reputation. The black lie is used to prevent people from knowing things they have every right to know, or to do deliberate harm to someone else. I have no truck with black lies; they make me very angry.

The white lie, on the other hand, is used to *avoid* hurting other people unnecessarily. I am busy teaching my children when, why, and how to tell white lies. My daughter Elizabeth, for instance, who is six, has the child's instinctive urge to lay it on the line. She has to be taught that it is not nice to say, upon opening a present from a grown-up relative or a friend of her own age, "Ugh, I hate this." At least, it mustn't be said in the presence of the giver. I am teaching her to say, "Oh, I don't have one of these." The fact that she wouldn't want one either is beside the point. At the very least, I tell her, she should be able to muster a simple "Thank you so much."

Elizabeth is going to need to know how to tell white lies if she wants to get through life without offending everyone in sight. All of us are constantly put into the position of having to avoid the total truth or be marked down as boorish and hurtful. We've all been to dinner parties where the hostess has overreached herself trying to gourmet things up and produced one sodden, inedible course after another. We are all asked to admire someone's latest purchase, whether it be clothes, furniture, or even a new house, that is in perfectly ghastly taste—according to our lights—or to comment on someone's performance at the local hospital benefit (embarrassing), or the poem he or she got published in the town newspaper (maudlin).

There is simply no point or percentage in telling people that they're lousy cooks, tone-deaf singers, or virtually illiterate. Sometimes, you can get away with saying nothing at all. But more often, you're going to have to say something, the person is standing right there, all expectant, and the nice thing to do is to draw on your repertoire of white lies. The beauty of the appropriate white lie is that it sidesteps the necessity of confronting someone else with the awful truth, but at the same time manages to avoid the kind of total untruth that will leave you feeling compromised, embarrassed, or guilty.

Let's examine three areas in which the white lie is especially useful or important.

1. Using the white lie to get out of something you don't want to do.
2. Using white lies to counter requests that you be completely frank.
3. Saving yourself with white lies when you think it's safe at last to be totally honest.

I'm So Sorry We Can't

Your friend Ellen calls to invite you for dinner on the twentieth. Ellen and her husband Sam are both interesting people, you've known them for years, and you have had some very good times together in the past. But there's a problem. Ellen and Sam are having severe marital problems. Last time you went to dinner at their place, they criticized one another's every move, yelled at one another several times, and worst of all, kept trying to get you to take sides anytime one or the other of them was out of the room. You are neither a marriage counselor nor a referee. You're fond of them both, and their fighting made you sad and uncomfortable. There's no way you're going to put yourself through another evening like that. People who can get into a rage over the fact that the mushrooms were left out of the salad or because the temperature of the cheese was too low need more help than you can offer.

You are tempted to be totally honest and say, "Look, Ellen, I'll see you after the divorce." But that would be cruel, might well bring on tears, would involve you even more in the mess she and Sam are making of their lives, and wouldn't be of any help to anyone, you included. Besides, they may patch it up and your comment would never be forgotten or forgiven.

Unfortunately, you have no good excuse. Your calendar is absolutely blank for the twentieth. That calendar, however, is your partial salvation. Everyone should take the precaution of building up in other people's minds the awareness that you never do anything without consulting your calendar. If you are a very busy person yourself, the fact that you have to consult your calendar will be accepted without question. If you're a person who is known to be something of a homebody, it's wise to create the impression that you have a mind like a sieve and can never remember dates. Never accept any invitation without consulting your calendar —because even the few seconds it takes to do that will give you time to think of excuses when you don't want to do something.

What excuse—what white lie—are you going to come up with? There are, of course, dozens of possibilities. You're already going out to dinner that night, you have people coming to dinner, it's not a good day because you have to get an especially early start the next morning, etc. You undoubtedly have favorites of your own. But you have to be careful. You have to remember that if there's any way your white lie can be found out, it will happen.

When you're using white lies to get out of something you

don't want to do, there are several guidelines to keep in mind.

1. Give your white lies some flesh.

It never works to say simply, "Oh, I'm sorry, we're busy that night," especially with anyone you know at all well. Rightly or wrongly, they won't believe you. They'll assume you don't want to come or are hoping something better will turn up. On the other hand, although it's important to give a specific excuse, fleshed out with a detail or two, you don't want to tell them too much. The more you say, the more you have to remember about what you said, and the more likely you are to get trapped later on.

2. Try to use a story that has at least some basis, however slight, in actual truth.

The reason for basing your white lie on at least a seed of truth is simple: it makes it easier to tell your story fluently and convincingly. For example, if you've just had a letter from your Aunt Margaret announcing that she and Uncle Todd expect to be driving through your part of the country next month, you can move up the date of their arrival to coincide with the date you're trying to get out of. Eventually, of course, you're going to try to ward off Aunt Margaret's visit itself. But that very fact gives you something to say in your current crisis: "Oh, I only wish we could. My Aunt Margaret is descending upon us, God forbid."

3. Get your white lies straight with everyone else in your household.

Make sure that your spouse, lover, roommate, or anyone else involved is fully apprised of *exactly* what you said to get out of an engagement. If you have children old enough to answer the telephone, make sure they know what the score is, too. You never know when somebody is actively going to check up on you, or even innocently ask how you liked the play you didn't go to. Have everybody prepared to deal with any such inquiries.

4. Always have a "future imperfect" white lie in reserve.

When you decline an invitation, many people will come back with, "Well, then, what night would you be free the following week?" Caught. But not if you're prepared. "Well," you can say, "Bob and I are going to try to get out of town for a few days either that week or the following one. It depends on what's going on at Bob's office, so we're not sure of our dates yet, but we're keeping that period open."

5. If you're really caught off guard by an invitation, stall.

As a last resort, you can always say, "I'll have to check with my wife (girl friend, roommate). She was saying something about trying to get tickets to a show, and I'm not sure where we're at." If you're single, you can fall back on the "overworked" ploy. "You know, I don't want to say yes and then let you down. We've got a big project coming up at the company that week, and I have the awful feeling it's going to mean a lot of late nights."

With these guidelines in mind, start working on your own perfect stories.

What Do You Really Think?

Whenever people ask you to give your frank opinion, beware. It's time for a white lie. It doesn't matter whether it's about their new hairdo, their current romantic interest, the job they've done on an office project, or the first two chapters of the novel they're writing at the kitchen table after dinner. They don't want the truth, they want reassurance. Oh, sure, they may be able to take a little constructive criticism provided your overall response is one of approval. But they don't want to hear anything that's more than one-tenth negative if they've got any stake in the matter at all.

As a nice person, you will avoid telling them what they don't want to hear. On the other hand you don't want to let yourself be trapped into giving wholehearted approval to someone or something about which you have severe reservations.

In trying to deal with such situations, one can learn a great deal from theater people—actors, actresses, producers, writers, and composers. Aside from lawyers, whose profession it is, no one group of people has as highly developed a knack for telling white lies as theater people. They need an extensive repertoire of white lies because the professional theater is one of the tightest little worlds in existence. Theater people are always going to see one another's performances. They may go out of envy, love, or sheer undying curiosity, but they go. That means, theater being as chancy, disaster prone, and volatile as it is, that theater people are constantly being put in the position of finding something nice to say about abject failure. And they're absolute wizards at it.

"I think that has to be your most challenging role." (Real Meaning: You're in over your head this time.)

"You looked absolutely radiant." (Real Meaning: The only decent thing about this show was the costumes.)

"The audience seemed to love it." (Real Meaning: The critics are going to murder you.)

"My dear, I've never seen anything like it." (Real Meaning: My God, what a travesty.)

The secret here, of course, is misdirection. Misdirection is just as applicable to the everyday situations we all find ourselves in. It simply means finding the one good thing you can say, no matter how insignificant, and focusing on that one aspect of the situation.

"The change is amazing." (Real Meaning: What butcher got hold of your hair?)

"Your daughter must have worked awfully hard on that Chopin piece." (Real Meaning: Buy that child a pair of handcuffs.)

"She seemed a little nervous, but she's awfully pretty."

(Real Meaning: You've gotten yourself tied up with a neurotic mess.)

"What wonderful bright colors." (Real Meaning: Too bad they're all on the same dress.)

So whenever anyone asks your frank opinion, latch onto the one good thing you can find to say, and under no circumstances tell them the truth. Keep your real meaning absolutely to yourself. Nobody really wants to hear it.

I Never Did Like Her

Even the nicest person, of course, gets the itch to be totally honest. This is especially true if you've been holding back an opinion of someone or something because you know that to say what you really believe is going to hurt someone else. But then suddenly the situation changes, and you think, "Now I can get it off my chest and instead of being hurtful the truth will actually help."

Don't do it. Just when you think it's finally safe to be honest is often the moment to show particular restraint.

My husband Joe had a friend from college days whom I'll call David. David had grown up with money, very old money, and had the kind of restrained dignified personality that seemed perfectly matched to his New England banking family background. But after his divorce from his equally restrained first wife, he went a little haywire and took up with a very pretty but raucous young thing who had grown up poor and feisty. She laughed too loudly and talked incessantly, and loved to tell dirty jokes. Joe was not at all fond of her.

One day David took his lady friend Marsha to his country club for the afternoon. He left her by the pool while he played a quick nine holes of golf. Marsha kept trying to strike up conversations, but got a very frosty reception from the assembled matrons. When David got back from his golf game, he got into a deep huddle about the economy with a fellow member, and Marsha began to get quite annoyed. She dove into the pool, swam to the shallow end and stood up, the water coming just barely above the level of her breasts. She then proceeded to take off both the top and the bottom of her bikini, waved them aloft and shouted, "Hey, David, wantta swim?"

David told this story to Joe over lunch a couple of weeks later, using it as an illustration of why he had broken up with Marsha. Aha, thought Joe, now I can be honest, and console David at the same time.

"Good for you," Joe said. "You're well rid of her. I always did think she was something of a twit."

"I know," said David, "I don't know how I ever got involved with her."

Joe didn't see David again for a month, and then ran into him at the theater. He asked David how he was doing.

"Very well," said David. "Marsha and I got together again. She should be along any minute, she just went to the ladies' room."

Joe, of course, would have liked to have disappeared into thin air.

So if you think everything has changed, and that at last you can be totally honest, always remember that everything can change right back again all too quickly.

There's another aspect to this kind of situation. This time, in very similar circumstances, it was I who got myself in trouble. A man I'd known for many years and who was a good friend broke up with a woman he'd been living with for two years. I'd always loathed the lady—who again, wasn't one—and I immediately launched into a long list of her failings, knocking her intelligence, her manners, and suggesting that she'd only been interested in my friend for his money. Midway through my tirade, I noticed that my old friend was looking rather pained, and I realized what I was doing. Okay, he'd broken up with her, but my comments were almost as insulting to him as they were to her. I was telling him, in essence, that he'd been a fool, had no taste in women, and, worst of all, that she wouldn't have been interested in him if it weren't for his money.

Thanks a lot.

So even if it seems that the time has rolled around for total honesty, the nice person will stop and think, wait, and keep his or her mouth shut.

What both Joe and I should have said was, "Oh, I'm sorry, it must be a hard time for you"—a white lie coupled with what was certainly the truth of the matter.

2

Knowing Your Audience

Nice people have the right to negative opinions.

The nice person has the right to dislike other people—a neighbor, co-worker, relative, or whoever. The nice person has the right to hold public figures in low esteem, whether it's a politician, entertainer, sports figure, or newspaper columnist. The nice person has the right to hate a hit movie or show, to find a best-selling book boring, or to think hockey is a game for animals.

But the nice person also has a responsibility to keep quiet about those negative opinions in certain circumstances. Because it's all too easy to embarrass yourself and others.

You may simply speak too quickly, as one woman did at a cultural fund raiser my husband attended recently. Joe was standing with a group of people, including this woman whom he'd never met before. Someone mentioned the Muppets. As it happens, Joe composed the music for "Sesame Street" and the feature movie "The Great Muppet Caper" starring Kermit and Miss Piggy. The woman in question was obviously un-aware of that fact, because she opened her mouth and said, "I think the Muppets are so dumb."

This is called being too fast on the draw. To begin with, she was ignoring the circumstances she found herself in. It was a *cultural* fund raiser, attended by many people from the world of television. Moreover, she didn't know several of the people in the group. Given the nature of the occasion, a definite possibility existed that one or more of these people might be somehow involved with "The Muppet Show." Finally, she didn't stop to think *why* the Muppets might have been mentioned in the first place. If she'd kept her mouth shut for another thirty seconds, she would have found out that Joe was involved creatively with Jim Henson and the Muppets, and, one assumes, would have had the good sense to keep her opinion to herself.

Joe, nicely, didn't say a word in response. People do have a right to their opinions, and he saw no reason to embarrass her. Another member of the group wasn't so reticent, however, and explained who Joe was.

"Oh dear," said the woman, "I've done it again."

She was, apparently, a chronic foot-in-mouther.

To avoid putting *your* foot in your mouth, there are three guidelines I'd like to explore:

1. Remember that it's a very small world.
2. Know your audience.
3. Observe the caution signs.

I Had No Idea He Was Your Brother-in-law

It's been estimated that in contemporary America none of us is more than five people away from almost anybody we might want to contact. That is, you know someone, who knows someone else, who is acquainted with a person who could put you in touch with a fourth party, who could get through to even the most famous VIP. At least that's the statistical probability. In practice, you'd probably run into a lot of dead ends along the way. But there's no question that we live in a surprisingly small world.

We may have largely abandoned the close, lifelong connectedness that was once the hallmark of small-town life, but the very mobility we've adopted has created new kinds of networks. Three friends who grow up together may scatter to different colleges, enter different professions, marry people from different parts of the country, settle down in one place for a few years only to move on eventually to another city or state. And as their lives unfold they inevitably create an extensive network of friends, acquaintances, and relatives. Marshall McLuhan was right on target when he coined the phrase "global village."

What does that mean in terms of being a nice person? It means be careful.

You never can tell whom somebody else is going to know. It's become commonplace to discover that we share an acquaintance with somebody we've just met. Coincidence is more and more the stuff of everyday life. Your dentist's sister may turn out to be married to the political columnist whose articles drive you into a rage; or that very "jiggly" actress on the new television series you loathe may be your next-door neighbor's best friend from college days. You never can tell.

Recognizing that it's a small world doesn't mean that you have to go around with a strip of masking tape over your mouth, though. It simply means that before you vent a negative opinion you should find out something about the person you are talking to. You need to know your audience.

Getting to Know You

With whom are you dealing? Who is your audience? We all exercise restraint when we're dealing with certain people because we know already how far we can go. We don't say f――― in front of grandmother (unless of course she's given to uttering the occasional Anglo-Saxonism herself). We don't boast about our new car to a neighbor who has lost a son in an automobile accident a few weeks earlier. We wisely avoid discussing politics with the boss when we know his or her leanings are considerably to the right or left of our own.

But often we find ourselves talking with people we haven't met before, or whom we don't know much about. What we have to do is carry on a conversation that stays away from potential trouble spots but at the same time will cause people to reveal something about themselves, so that we can begin to get a fix on who they are. It's always been claimed that the weather is the safest topic under the sun, but it's also useless, because you're not going to learn anything about the person that's helpful in assessing them. The fact that somebody is especially fond of the fall doesn't give you much to work on.

At the other extreme, politics, religion, and sex are always dangerous topics. I will never forget the young woman who, within two minutes of having been introduced to Joe and me, revealed that she was bisexual, and began to discuss her life-style at some length. Bisexuality is very "in" these days, in some circles, and perhaps she was trying to show how liberated and "with it" she was. But I am doubtful that passionate declarations on sex, politics, or religion are ever the way to a stranger's heart. That kind of approach seems appropriate only to situations where it's vital to get to the sticking point in a hurry—in singles bars, perhaps.

I find that the safest, and at the same time most efficient

method of discovering *who* you're talking to—what they're like as people—is to focus on the what, when, or where of the circumstances you find yourself in. You're both at the same business convention, the same party, traveling on the same plane—it doesn't really matter where you are, you are already sharing something in common by occupying the same space. Your initial comment on that shared space should be positive in most cases. "Quite a convention." Or, "Sheila does know how to give a party." On an airplane, it is always permissible to be negative, wondering when, if ever, you're going to take off.

A simple remark like, "Sheila does know how to give a party," can quickly produce a lot of information in return. You may discover that it's the first time the person you're talking to has been invited (which tells you that you know Sheila better than he or she does); that the person wouldn't dare give such a large party without a caterer like Sheila's (aha, you suddenly know something about the person's economic status); or that the person is Sheila's niece visiting from Indianapolis (a family connection, be very careful).

It's only fair, of course, to give back some information in return. But the nice person isn't required to give away more than he or she is getting. If the answers you are getting are vague or reticent, don't hesitate to be equally vague. Vagueness, indeed, is the nice person's first line of defense. If the person you're talking to doesn't want to cooperate in this exchange of particulars, the nice person has every right to maintain a certain distance. Or, for that matter, to beat a physical retreat, if possible. If you're sitting next to someone on a plane, you can't very well do that without a parachute, but you can open a magazine and begin to read. The nice person has no responsibility for pursuing a dead-end conversation except in a professional capacity, as teacher, doctor, lawyer or, as has too often been my own experience, as a television interviewer.

If matters are progressing easily, however, it will soon be time to move into the area of opinion. Although everyone seems far too eager and too quick to express an opinion these days, and by so doing often put both feet in their mouths, no genuine interaction between human beings can continue for long without opinions being expressed. Opinions are what make conversations and people interesting. Opinions also make it possible to find out who you are really talking to. But there are some subjects that on a first encounter are much safer than others. Movies, television shows, entertainers, sports and, in some circles, even books are subjects open to discussion on a reasonably rational level—unlike politics, religion, and sex.

That's not to say that you should come on too strong at the start. The world is full of fanatics, people who virtually burst into flame if you suggest that the latest Woody Allen movie or Barbra Streisand performance isn't up to par. It doesn't matter how many bouquets you've thrown in the past, the slightest criticism can produce an incendiary reaction. I know—I have hundreds of letters in the CBS files to prove it.

That's why I ask people I've just met what *they* think of a movie, a book, or whatever, rather than telling them what I think. And the answer gives you more clues as to who your audience is, and what the person is actually like. Some people lead very busy lives, or don't want to stand in long lines, and may not get around to seeing a movie or show immediately. But if, after six months or so, you ask people if they've seen a big hit and they look at you blankly, you know immediately that you've mentioned a subject in which they have no interest. If they say they haven't seen it but want to very much, they will almost invariably come back by discussing a movie or play they have seen. And you've learned something about them. The same is true with sports. Mention a hot team—baseball, basketball, football, depending upon the season—and see what happens. From the reaction you get you can paint in another corner of the individual's emerging portrait.

Food is the best topic of all to use in trying to draw people out. Everybody has to eat to survive, but there are all kinds of eaters; it is a universal subject that everyone responds to in slightly different ways. You can find out very quickly that someone looks upon food primarily as fuel for the body, that someone else is a gourmet, that another person is dieting or fasting or follows a vegetarian regime. And the subject of food easily leads into such topics as exercise, jogging, health in general, and may spill over into a discussion of food stamps or school lunches. With a great rush, you're learning a great deal about the person's life-style, prejudices, and enthusiasms.

Of course, if you want to debate people on any of these subjects, that is your privilege, but you'll be debating them on the basis of some knowledge of who they are and what their point of view is, and whether or not they're rational or irrational on the subject. Once you know who your audience is, you're free to proceed as you will. If you offend them, at least it will be on the basis of some idea of who they are and what they believe. Instead of putting your foot in your mouth you will be taking issue. And those are two very different things.

Caution Signs

Sometimes, of course, it's very difficult to keep one's mouth shut. For all of us, there are people and subjects whose mere mention causes us to blurt out our feelings.

A year ago, for example, I attended a small Los Angeles dinner party given by a prominent film producer and his wife. I'll call them the Renfields. Among the half-dozen guests was the wife of a prominent musician. She was known for her aggressiveness, but on this particular evening she surpassed herself.

While we were having cocktails, the names of a New York-based couple in the film business were mentioned, and the musician's wife immediately began tearing them to shreds with the ferocity of a tigress disemboweling her prey. The rest of us were horrified, since we knew that the couple she was attacking were very close friends of our hosts. The Renfields at first sat in stunned silence and then tried, politely, to defend their friends—but that only seemed to encourage the woman's vitriolic outburst. Others of us tried to change the subject, without success. In the end, we all started side conversations with one another, and the woman, finally realizing that she'd lost her audience, subsided. The atmosphere remained uneasy, however, for the remainder of the evening. A party had been spoiled.

To give the woman the benefit of the doubt, let's assume that she was unaware of the close relationship between the Renfields and the couple she was saying so many dreadful things about. If so, nevertheless she was ignoring the fact that it's a very small world, and that one has to learn something about one's audience before making strong negative statements.

But what particularly struck me was the way she ignored all the caution signs that the rest of us were figuratively hoisting aloft. It should have been immediately apparent to her that she was traversing dangerous ground. To begin with, there was the absolute silence that settled over the room. Several of us shifted uncomfortably in our chairs. There were nervous coughs. Cigarettes were puffed on with telltale force. Yet she ignored all these caution signs. The fact that the Renfields began to defend the couple in question, however politely, should have served as a definite red light. But she just kept speeding along, getting herself into deeper and deeper trouble.

Caution signs can, of course, be very subtle—hidden in the underbrush, as it were. But even such subtle signs as a slight frown, a small motion of the hand, or a momentary edge to the voice, can be caught and understood in terms of the context of the situation if you are prepared for them. The best way to be prepared to read them is actually to elicit those signs by using the "Getting To Know You" techniques.

All you have to do is to identify the person or subject you're about to hold forth on and then STOP.

Never begin with your opinion when you don't know who your audience is.

If the other person has neutral or negative feelings about the individual or subject you've identified, you will get an indifferent reply, a cautious one, or, if the person himself or herself is incautious, a negative reply.

If the other person has strong positive feelings about the individual or subject you've mentioned, he or she will almost invariably say so in no uncertain terms: "Oh, do you know Janet? Terrific lady, isn't she?"

In fact you may not think Janet is so terrific at all. But now you know that you're going to get yourself in trouble if you give your true opinion. Not only are you likely to create an embarrassing situation at the moment, but your criticism of Janet may well get back to her. It's time to do a sidestep.

Having brought up Janet's name, however, you're going to have to say *something* about her. I find that the easiest way to sidestep the issue is to rack your brain and come up with some vaguely positive or at least innocuous comment about Janet, and then to immediately add that you don't know her very well or haven't seen her in some time.

You can say Janet's very pretty, or that she seems very

smart, or that she's obviously very successful, or seems to work so hard—there are endless variations on the vague compliment.

Then say that you don't know her all that well or have rather lost contact, and change the subject.

By changing the subject, you are issuing your own signal, waving your own cautionary flag, and reducing the possibility of getting into any further discussion of Janet's virtues or, as you see it, defects.

The nice person has a right to negative opinions.

But by keeping in mind that it's a very small world, getting to know your audience before you state those negative opinions, and observing the caution signs along the way, you will not only be behaving in a nice way but also keeping your foot out of your mouth.

3

Keeping It Private, or "This Is Your Life"

People are naturally curious about other people. And that's fine. One of the ways we define ourselves is by comparing our own experiences and feelings with those of others.

But, unfortunately, a lot of people are more than just curious: they're plain nosey. They want to know things that are none of their business.

They want to know how much you earn.

They want to know if you're sleeping with that new guy you're seeing.

They want to know exactly what you were in the hospital for last week.

They want to know why your marriage is on the rocks.

And if you don't tell them of your own accord, they'll ask you such questions point blank. In my opinion, the nice person simply shouldn't ask such questions, but these days even a great many otherwise very nice people have gotten the idea that it's perfectly okay to ask you practically anything. That's another delusion we have the Age of Total Honesty to thank for. "I'm perfectly willing to tell all," people apparently say to themselves, "so why shouldn't you be?"

In general, just as women tend to be franker than men, they also tend to be more overtly nosey. Perhaps that's a matter of societal conditioning, but I suspect that it also has something to do with the fact that as childbearers and mothers, women are dealing with a more personal context to begin with. The woman who is pregnant for the first time, for example, may have a great need to compare notes, in order to determine whether some of the extraordinary things that are happening to her body are normal or abnormal. And most women are more than willing to share their own private histories in that regard. They are willing to do so because they are imparting a form of knowledge that other women genuinely need to have.

The need to know is, I think, the crux of the matter here. Television news organizations decide the makeup of a given broadcast, the stories they are going to cover, in considerable measure on the basis of "the public's need to know." There is a great deal of debate about this question, of course. Many commentators on the quality of television, and millions of television viewers, question whether we really need to know as much as we're told about the latest ax murder, kidnapping, or plane crash. Nevertheless, imperfect a criterion though it may be, I think the concept of the need to know is also extremely useful in determining what questions we're going to answer, and which ones we're going to sidestep, in our daily lives.

For instance, if a pregnant friend asks me about my physical, or in some cases psychological, experiences while I was carrying Elizabeth or Andrew, I'll be happy to tell her anything I can. But if she goes on from that to ask me about Joe's and my sex life during my pregnancies, I draw the line. First of all it is none of her business, and second, it's not necessarily going to be helpful information—indeed, it might even be harmful, causing her to compare her husband unfavorably to Joe. Human sexual practices vary so much from person to person and couple to couple, and are affected by so many complex individual psychological factors, that my particular experiences are nothing she needs to know. If she's worried about her sex life during pregnancy, or having problems, then she needs to consult a professional who can draw upon a knowledge of the case histories of hundreds of women.

Thus, whenever I am asked a personal question, I silently consider the matter of the person's need to know the answer. Obviously, there are questions one answers when they're asked by a very close friend that one wouldn't answer when asked by somebody else. But more often the dilemma arises of how to refuse to answer, gracefully and nicely.

I'd like to look at that dilemma in three contexts:

1. Dealing with gossip mongers.
2. Money matters.
3. The parent trap.

Spreading the News

A young woman at ABC whom I was close to was having an affair with a newscaster who was a married man. The nature of Linda's and Stan's relationship was fairly common knowledge among the news staffers. People didn't sit around and discuss it at length, but minor comments were made from time to time. Because it was such common knowledge, I assumed that Linda and Stan were being very open about it, and didn't give a damn what people thought.

My assumption was wrong.

One day when I ran into Linda, I said, quite offhandedly, "Hi, Linda, how are things with Stan?"

Linda immediately turned scarlet and stammered, "I don't know what, what you're talking about." And then she virtually fled. From then on, Linda avoided me. I knew her secret. A great many other people did too, of course, but I was one of the few who had, quite innocently, made it clear to her that I knew.

Unquestionably, Linda was being naive. But I think a great many nice people are naive when it comes to realizing that other people gossip constantly, and that once a secret of any real interest gets out, it's going to be spread around very quickly. Nice people, who pride themselves on their ability to keep confidences, and are careful about repeating gossip too loosely, make the mistake of assuming that other people do the same.

The truth is that there are a great many people in this world who take pleasure in spreading any story they can get their hands on, and who couldn't keep a confidence under threat of death. Nice people, in a word, have to watch out. That's why it's important to know how to avoid answering nosey questions about oneself. I think the nice person has to go on the assumption that anything he or she reveals has a very good chance of being repeated.

In certain areas of your life, of course, you may not care at all what people know. Everybody knows, for instance, that Joe and I get into fairly strenuous debates about a variety of subjects from time to time. And neither Joe nor I could care less. We always end up laughing about our debates, and everybody knows that, too, since Joe and I kid one another and ourselves about it a lot. But another couple, whose outward relationship has always appeared serene, but who have been having their troubles lately and begun fighting a good deal, may not want to have the world know that at all.

Suppose that such a couple, Sid and Eileen, have a loud argument one Tuesday night. Sid has even thrown a glass across the room which shattered in the fireplace. The sounds of the argument, and the crashing of the glass in particular, were heard by the couple's downstairs neighbors and friends, Bob and Gloria. The next day, Eileen runs into Gloria in the lobby of the apartment building, and Gloria asks, "Is everything okay with you and Sid?"

In my opinion, Gloria shouldn't ask this question in the first place. It may be that she's genuinely concerned, and wants to help, but things haven't reached such a pass that she should be actively intervening at this point. (There are times when intervention is necessary, as I'll be discussing in a later chapter.) It really should be Eileen's place to tell Gloria what's going on if she wants to.

But the question has been asked. How can Eileen deal with it? Eileen in fact has a double problem, in that Gloria is a considerable gossip. If Eileen simply replies, "Fine, of course," she knows perfectly well that Gloria's going to be marching around saying, "Sid and Eileen are having some kind of problem, but she won't even talk about it." And that will pave the way for other people to speculate on the nature of the problem. Such speculation may in fact end up making the problem seem a lot worse than it is.

The way to deal with this kind of situation is to make a partial admission, but to make light of it. One way of making light of it is to bounce the ball back into the other person's court. Eileen could say, for example, "Of course everything's okay. Haven't you and Bob ever had a spat?"

Since every couple in the world has at least the occasional spat, Gloria is put on the defensive. Now, if she's really determined to get the true story, and to hell with being nice, Gloria might come back with, "Well, yes, but very quiet ones."

What Eileen needs now is a general comment about life. "Oh, Gloria, don't you know it's important to let your feelings out," ought to do the trick.

Real dyed-in-the-wool gossip mongers, unfortunately, will

be much more aggressive than Gloria. They make a career of betraying trusts, constantly passing on things that were told them in confidence. And they try to draw other people into their web by trading something they know (and weren't supposed to tell) for something they want to know from you (and will certainly trade for another piece of information later). It's absolutely necessary to be tough with them. Once you are on to such a person, you should refuse to listen to their stories. You have to be blunt about it and say right out, "I really don't want to hear this." If they ask you something, like, "What were you in the hospital for?"—a question no nice person should *ever* ask—I would recommend replying, "I can't think of a more boring subject, my dear. How have *you* been?"

Of course, a lot of very nice people may also want to know why you're in the hospital. They're not gossip mongers, they're good friends. And if you want to go into it, that's up to you. But I think it's better to downplay the problems involved. For one thing, even nice people, once they hear your saga, are all too likely to come back at you with some horror story about someone they know who went through the "same thing." Telling you such a story is misguided niceness at its height. The person is trying to make you feel better by proving to you that things could be much worse, but if you're anything like me, such stories are only going to give you something more to worry about.

For that reason, I said as little as possible when I was suddenly hospitalized a month before the birth of my son Andrew because of hemorrhaging. When friends called to ask what they could do, and to inquire about my condition, I told them that it was nothing more than a little hemorrhaging, and that everything was fine, but that as a precaution I was going to stay in the hospital. In fact, everything wasn't all right. I was suffering from *placenta previa,* an intra-partum complication that in many cases can affect the health of the baby. The doctors wanted me to carry Andrew as close to term as possible, and there was considerable anxiety about the situation. But I didn't want to talk about those problems. There seemed to me nothing to be gained by it. I would only succeed in worrying our friends, and I certainly wanted to avoid hearing any tales about women who'd had similar problems. When anyone pressed me about my condition, I said, "I really don't want to dwell on it, there's no point in that," and changed the subject. Even after Andrew was safely born, I didn't elaborate. The crisis was over—why discuss it? I'm still uncomfortable about it, but the story does have its point here.

Thus, while inquiring after someone's health when he or she is ill is not only acceptable but a nice thing to do, the nice person will avoid pressing for details. If the ill friend or relative wants to go into detail, nothing will stop them, you can be sure—in fact, you may end up wishing you hadn't asked.

There is another private area, however, about which I think it's completely *unacceptable* to make inquiries: you guessed it, sex. Thanks, or no thanks, to the sexual revolution, a great many people seem to think it's as permissible to ask about your sex life as to inquire about what you had for dinner last night. If someone starts prying into your sex life, past or present, the nice way to deflect such questions is to say, "You know, you really shouldn't ask that kind of thing. Some people might get very upset." You thus manage to suggest that even though you're not going to take serious offense, you have no intention of answering, either. In this area, though, I wouldn't hesitate to say, "That's none of your business."

Of course, if you feel comfortable discussing sex, as many people do these days, or want to boast, which even more people do, go right ahead. Just remember that you're not just telling the person sitting opposite you the who, the what, and the how many times of it—you're telling the world, in the long run. Despite today's casual attitude about sex in many quarters, it still makes the juiciest gossip going.

The Root of All Status

"How much do you earn at CBS, Pat?"

I've been asked that question dozens of times. I think it's a very rude question, but I'm not surprised that it gets asked so often. Our society, after all, is the most acquisitive, materialistic, and commercialized on earth. Americans are obsessed with money, which is perfectly natural since it's one of the few lasting measures of status we have. We have no royalty, we elevate and then discard our politicians, entertainers, and sports stars with both casual and callous abandon. And, as a society, we aren't much impressed by intellectual achievement. So money is about all that's left.

What's more, a great many people are happy to have the world know what they earn. Golf and tennis pros, jockeys and race car drivers compete like mad to win the title of leading money winner for a season. And the standings are regularly printed, in precise dollars and cents, in magazines and newspapers, and announced on television. You can read in the papers every day what people are making, the pitcher who's just signed for $800,000 a year, the entertainer who's getting $200,000 for one night in Las Vegas, the corporate chairman who's just been hired at $500,000 a year with another $300,000 in stock thrown in to sweeten the deal. If you pay any attention to contract disputes, you can also figure out exactly what your neighbor the teacher or fire fighter is making a year.

Fine. If it's public knowledge, it's public knowledge. But if it isn't public knowledge, it generally means that the individual concerned doesn't want it to be. To ask someone to his or her face what he or she is making seems to me extremely pushy. But how, if you feel the same way, can you deflect the question without blatantly saying, "That's none of your business"?

When I'm asked the question, I smile and reply, "Well, a lot more than a cancer researcher at New York University and a lot less than some baseball players who keep dropping fly balls in left field." And then I add, "Of course, the cancer researcher ought to be making more than me or the left fielder, but that doesn't seem to be the way things work."

I've found this answer to be 100 percent effective. There really is no way anyone can press you to be more specific without appearing totally obnoxious. What's more, a point has been made about money in general that can lead into other conversational areas concerning the values we place on certain kinds of work. Or, on a simpler level, the other person has the option of talking about the left fielder in question or a story he or she saw about what's going on in the field of cancer research. The conversation hasn't been brought to a halt, it's been opened up.

That answer won't work, of course, if your own salary is likely to be less than that cancer researcher's. In those circumstances, I'd make a joke of it, saying, "I'm well above the poverty line." A somewhat flippant answer of this kind makes it clear to the questioner that a serious reply isn't going to be forthcoming. My mother has always told me that I should resist my urge to make a joke of things, but I find that it's often the most effective way to defuse a tricky situation.

And then there's that other, absolutely ubiquitous money question: "How much did you pay for that?"

There are three reasons why people ask that question.

1. They want one themselves and they want to find out if they can afford it or think it's worth the price.

2. They have one themselves already and they want to find out if you got a better or worse deal than they did.

3. They're obsessed with money.

The first of these three reasons is perfectly honorable in the broad sense. But the nicer way to go about getting the desired information is to begin by asking you where you bought it, rather than how much it cost. That gives you the opportunity to say how much it cost if you are willing to do so. If not, since the questioner knows where it can be obtained, he or she can go price it at the source.

In deciding whether or not *you* want to say how much something cost, I think the major consideration is what the something is. Appliances, electrical gadgets, sports equipment, and dozens of other everyday family purchases pose no problem, as I see it. After all, we're talking about standard brand items that are available everywhere, with their prices constantly being advertised. There's no reason to be secretive about these kinds of goods.

On the other hand, if someone asks you what a new dress, a piece of jewelry, or a fur coat cost, it begins to be a different matter, I, for one, begin to suspect the motivation here. In the case of a dress, for example, it seems unlikely that the woman who asks you its cost really wants one "just like it" for herself—and if she does, you'd rather she didn't have it, you bought it because it suits your taste and makes you look good, and you don't want to run into it on someone else at every other party. It may be that even your husband or live-in lover doesn't know what the dress cost and you're not about to let the cat out of the bag. (Men, it should be said, also buy things for themselves and keep the price a secret.)

So you have to ask yourself why the person really wants to know what personal items like clothes or jewelry cost, especially when they are clearly fairly expensive. In most cases, I think the person is really trying to find out how extravagant you are. And the nice person has no obligation to reveal that. It may be that in other areas you're very frugal, and the cost of the dress is going to be misleading as an indication of how high off the hog you're living. Besides, it's nobody else's business.

There are several replies I use to deflect questions about the cost of personal items. The easiest way out is to say, "I have no idea, it was a present." It's a wise idea to identify the giver (fictional or otherwise): husband, wife, parents, whoever. That's to avoid giving the impression that you have a secret admirer. The "it was a present" approach can work with a host of items from a woman's string of pearls to a man's digital watch. When something is unlikely to have been a present (an evening gown, say), I take another tack, replying, "Much less than you'd think. I got it on sale." That usually stops people, but if they persist, you can say, "Oh, I think sale prices should always be a secret, don't you? It adds a little mystery to life." And of course you must smile a Cheshire Cat smile.

If your questioner is after bigger game, wanting to know how much rent you pay, or the cost of your new car, new house, or your recent winter vacation, there is really only one possible dodge: Raising your eyes to heaven, say, "Don't even ask. I'd rather not think about it."

What's more, that's likely to be a perfectly true statement.

The Parent Trap

Finally, I'd like to take a brief look at the problem (and advisability) of keeping it private when it comes to dealing with your own parents. The nature of the relationship is such that most parents are going to continue asking their adult children questions about themselves that may have been perfectly appropriate during the teenage years but no longer are when the son or daughter is in their twenties or older.

While some parents and their adult children may be particularly close to one another and particularly open with one another, and are fortunate to have such relationships, the myth of the son or daughter who tells his or her parents "everything" is just that—a myth. What's more, you can be absolutely certain that your parents haven't told you "everything" either. Everybody goes through the strange experience of discovering, later in life or even after a parent's death, that there was quite a lot going on we didn't know about.

Not only are there going to be a number of things your parents have never told you about themselves, the truth is that there are a lot of things they'd rather not know about you. That's true even when they ask leading questions which are touching on an area you want to keep private. Few parents really want to know that their career-successful daughter had an abortion last year, or that their son is having an affair with someone other than his wife. Despite the consciousness raising of recent years, many parents don't really want to know that a son or daughter is gay—or at least not any more about it than is absolutely necessary.

But they ask all these *questions,* you protest. Of course they do, but they only want one kind of answer, usually a negative one. "No, Mother, I did not have an abortion." "No, Father, I'm not cheating on Ellen." "No, Dad, Bob and I are just roommates."

So if you can't give them a no when they start prying, sidestep the issue. Tell a few white lies. Believe me, they'll usually make it easy for you to avoid the whole truth. They're well aware that some things are better kept private. They've been doing it themselves for a generation or two longer than you have.

4

I Hate to Ask You to Do This, But...

Being a nice person has its drawbacks as well as its satisfactions and rewards. One of the major drawbacks is that people are going to try to take advantage of your niceness and ask you to do things for them that they wouldn't ask other people to do The person who has a reputation for being nice is going to be requested to do favors, give of his or her money, time, and expertise, and be generally imposed upon.

The nice person is going to be asked to get other people tickets to the theater, football games, and rock concerts because, "I know you have the connections." The nice person is going to be asked by friends to "get it for me wholesale" because you happen to be in the business. You're going to be asked to give money to every charity there is, and to serve on one committee after another. If you have a special talent, you're going to be asked to play the piano or sing at other people's parties, cook dinner at other people's houses, or whip up a dress out of the bolt of silk a friend brought back from Japan. People are going to beg you to find their kids summer jobs, recommend them for college, or give them a free course in real estate or computer programming. In fact, any favor you could conceivably be asked to do, any responsibility that falls within your bailiwick, you can be sure you'll be requested to undertake.

The nice person can get exhausted.

The nice person has to learn to say no—nicely, of course.

The nice person should always keep in mind that just because you *can* do it doesn't mean you have to do it, or even should do it.

But since other people know or assume you can do it, how are you going to get out of it, how are you going to refuse to do irksome favors?

I'd like to examine how to avoid being imposed upon in several areas:

1. How to avoid becoming a "connection."
2. How to avoid being forced into charity.
3. How to avoid giving away your talents or expertise for free.
4. How to give a recommendation without doing it.

I Just Know You Can Help Me

A while back, one of my assistants at "CBS Morning News" said to me, "You know, Pat, this office is turning into a ticket brokerage."

"I know," I replied. "It's got to stop."

So many friends and acquaintances inside and outside CBS had been calling me asking if I could get them tickets to hit Broadway shows that the real work of my office wasn't getting done. The people who asked me to get them tickets were making two assumptions, in most cases. The first assumption was that because I reviewed Broadway shows and often interviewed their stars, I had the connections to get tickets, good tickets, even to sold-out musicals. This first assumption was to a considerable extent correct. Either through personal contacts or by using the clout that all the networks have in the entertainment world, it was often possible to get tickets for hot shows. A lot of people also made a second assumption—that I could get the tickets for free. On that, they were dead wrong. The critics get free tickets to opening nights, and that's it.

Explaining that fact was awkward in itself, and certainly no help in avoiding the task of getting the tickets. People didn't want me to think they'd called me just because they thought they could get "freebies," and so the inevitable reply was, "Oh, we don't mind paying for them, we just thought you could get us better seats." Of course, that still meant that I had to pay for them in the first place and keep an accounting of who owed me what. Then I had to put my staff to work on acquiring the tickets, which distracted them from the real business of preparing a five-day-a-week segment for the morning news. It was getting thoroughly out of hand.

And so I began saying no. To some people, I said, "Things are crazy around here this week, and I don't know if we'll have even five minutes to get around to it." And then, to make sure the person calling wouldn't think that he or she was alone in being turned down, I'd add, "I've already had to beg off on this twice today." When you're saying no to a request, I always think it's a good idea to convey that you're turning down other people too, whether it's true or not. Saying that can save a lot of hurt feelings.

Another tack I took was to say, "House seats to that show are completely unavailable, and I think you'd do just as well on your own. I wouldn't want to stick you with lousy seats. You might want to wait awhile instead of taking what's available now." That puts the ball back in their court. It also saves you from the annoyance that might arise if you did indeed get them lousy seats. When people assume that you have connections, they expect you to come up with the very best for them, and if you don't they're going to be mad at you. It's a case of the old saying, "No good deed ever goes unpunished."

Because of the nature of my job, what I get asked for is theater tickets. But it really doesn't matter what field you're in, there are always going to be people who will think you can get something for them for free, do it more easily or better than they can, and, the bottom line, save them the trouble of doing it themselves. If you're a plumber, your next-door neighbor is going to ask you to pick up a new faucet for him "since you'll be going to the supply store anyway." If you're a secretary, somebody is bound to ask you to photocopy a pile of stuff for them at the office "when you've got a free moment." And then there's the more generalized, "Oh, you're driving to the country tomorrow—could you bring me back a couple of bushels of apples?" Or, "Oh, you're flying back through Paris—could you pick up a bottle of perfume for me at the duty-free shop?"

Well, maybe you could do these things, and if you genuinely want to, more power to you. But if you'd really rather not, don't think you're going to lose your credentials as a nice person by refusing. If you can give a good practical reason why you can't, you're free and clear. On that trip to Europe, for instance, you can always say that you're changing planes, and it's a very tight turnaround in Paris, and you doubt if there'll be time to get to the duty-free shop. If you're asked to do photocopying, you can say that they've really clamped down at the office, and you can't get away with doing outside stuff anymore. The practical excuse doesn't have to be the whole truth, of course, so long as it sounds reasonable.

Sometimes, a good practical excuse is hard to come by.

In those circumstances, the "time element" dodge can be effective. The plumber can say, "Well, it always takes them half an hour to dig out single items like that, and I've got people screaming for my services all over town. Everybody's pipes seem to have burst at once." Or, more generally, "Well, I'll be glad to do it, but it's likely to be several days before I can get around to it."

When you're dealing with people who are particularly insistent, sometimes it's best to say, "Oh, that should be no problem." Then let it go for a day and call back to tell them there's a problem after all. People may be out of town, or booked solid, or are out of stock on that. Use whatever problem seems appropriate. The thing is that you are showing them you've *tried* (even if you haven't), and you can be almost 100 percent certain that the people who asked the favors won't check up on you. They asked you in the first place because they couldn't do whatever it was for themselves, or were too nervous to do it, or too lazy to do it. If you've tried and failed, they're not going to pursue it further on their own.

Sometimes the nice person, in order to preserve his or her sanity and keep from being inundated with requests for assistance, has to be a little devious. The only alternative to being devious in some situations is to say, "I really can't do that for you," a reply that is almost certain to be taken as meaning you don't want to and won't, which will give offense. Deviousness is better.

We're Counting on Your Contribution

People who want your contributions always tell you they're counting on you. They're counting on your twenty-five dollars for the United Fund, they're counting on your five-hundred-dollar gift to the college development fund, they're counting on you to contribute two cakes to the church bazaar. This is called counting your chickens before they're hatched. It's also a none too subtle form of blackmail—if you don't deliver, everybody's going to know that you can't be counted on, and are an unfeeling tightwad to boot.

The more prominent or seemingly affluent you are, the greater the number of organizations that are going to be counting on you, and the greater the dollar amount they're going to have put down next to your name in advance as an appropriate contribution. It doesn't matter what economic level you live on, in fact, you are always going to find yourself counted on for a lot more than you can afford to give. That necessarily means giving less than is expected and in many cases not giving at all.

There are a great many important and worthwhile charities, organizations, and institutions in this country that need and deserve help. For the nice person this presents a real dilemma. Wanting very much to help, the nice person ends up feeling guilty for not having done more, while other people who don't give a damn or a dollar are totally untroubled. That isn't fair. The nice person is usually especially generous as a matter of course, and shouldn't be made to feel lousy for not doing still more But if you're going to avoid giving more than you can afford or taking on more than you can realistically do to help, you've got to have some defenses that make it possible to say no without feeling guilty.

At CBS, as at so many large corporations across the country, an organized drive soliciting funds for the "United Way" is mounted every year. I myself am a "United Way" fund raiser. But I always try to keep in mind that people may really not be able to afford to give very much, or even anything at all. One person may be paying large medical bills for an ill parent, another may have three kids in college. As a fund raiser, I realize that people may not want to tell you why they can't contribute very much or not at all, and I don't believe in putting on too much pressure, worthy as the cause is. But what if someone does put pressure on you? How can you respond?

When someone calls on the telephone, accosts you at the office, or approaches you on the church steps and asks you to give to one cause or another, always allow them to get through their spiel, even if you know instantly that you're not going to contribute. These people care, they're giving of their time to solicit funds, and if you cut them off in mid-sentence you're putting them down. Once they've completed their pitch, don't jump right in and say no. Above all, never say, "Oh, I don't believe in that," or worse, "I'm sorry but I don't like the way your organization handles its funds." There are some organizations whose after-expenses charitable take is lower than it ought to be, but there's no point in attacking their credibility even if that's your real reason for not giving.

What you should say is, "I know that's a worthwhile cause, but . . ." By telling them it's a worthwhile cause, you at least avoid making them feel they've wasted their breath completely. As to what follows the "but," there are a number of possibilities. You can say, "We're putting everything into the cancer fund this year," or the heart fund, or whatever your choice may be. This suggests a particularized commitment that's hard to argue with. You can also say that you're strapped this year but hope to be able to help next year. That approach, however, has to be considered in the context of your life-style and the amount you're being asked to give. If your income is modest, you can say you're strapped even when you're being asked to contribute only a small amount. But if you live fairly luxuriously, that will work only when you're being approached about a major gift.

An increasing number of institutions and organizations these days try to get you to pledge larger amounts by giving you the option of spreading out your payments over the course of a year or more. Colleges and universities mounting major capital fund drives often use this technique. The temptation is to say, okay, okay, in order to get the fund raiser off your back, and then to forget to make the payments. But I think it's much better and more honest to say, "Look, I don't want to make a promise I can't keep," and get your pledge down to a level you know you can live with.

Finally, there are situations where you can offer something else instead. You can give old clothes or stored furniture to the neighborhood or church bazaar. You can offer to make telephone calls or lick envelopes. But if your time is precious—and for most of us these days, time is very definitely money—the best way out is to give a token amount, however small. Identify it as a token, say you'd like to do more, and suggest that every penny counts. Every penny does count, of course. And more to the point, the person who has approached you can check you off as having given *something,* however modest. That will make the fund raiser feel better.

But always remember that if you want to or have to say no, that's your right. Do it nicely, and don't feel guilty about it.

Since You're the Expert

As a well-known composer, Joe is constantly being asked to give his opinion of other people's attempts at musical composition. It may be the son of a friend or even an acquaintance whose efforts Joe is asked to comment on; the kid has formed his own rock band and cut a 45 RPM demonstration record. Somebody else's wife, a former model, has been taking singing lessons and wants a free appraisal and advice on how to break into musical theater. A friend from college days is a stockbroker but has long harbored the fantasy that he's got it in him to write a Broadway show—a package of his songs arrives in the mail.

I get it, too, although less often than Joe does. Friends want me to spend "an hour or so" advising a son or daughter who's in his or her last year of college on how to break into television news. Anybody who has any kind of expertise at all—and that means most of us—is going to be asked to give free advice. It happens to lawyers, accountants, chefs, stockbrokers, police officers, nurses, you name it.

"I have this little legal problem." "Can you show me how to make really light puff pastry?" "How can I get Bobby into the Police Academy?" Some questions or requests can be taken care of in five minutes, and the expert may be perfectly willing to do so. But reading through forty pages of a musical score, teaching someone to make puff pastry, or spending "an hour or so" discussing the television news business with junior are entirely another matter.

During most of the year, I have to attend several screenings of films, sometimes as many as three or four in a single day, attend two or three opening nights, set up location interviews, and go out with a crew to tape them, and show up at the studio at the crack of dawn five days a week. Sounds glamorous, I know, which is part of the problem; people think my work must be terrific fun. Well, it is fun, and I love it, but it is also extremely hard and often exhausting work. I also have a family to raise, and a husband I want to spend some time with alone. I do not have "an hour or so" available to give a crash course in newscasting to anybody; if I did it for the number of people who ask, I wouldn't even begin to get my job done. It's the same for anybody. Joe is always involved in several musical projects at once, any professional chef works ten or more hours a day six days a week as it is, and a good lawyer has undoubtedly got briefs piled up on his or her desk like cordwood. None of us, and millions of people like us, have the time to give free advice. But this doesn't stop people from asking, and nice ways have to be found to avoid taking on a lot of chores that are sheer imposition.

While the truth of the matter may be that you simply don't have the time, that's not a good thing to tell people. Friends assume that if you really wanted to you could make the time, and the fact that you're not willing to do that is seen as an indication that you're not as good a friend, or as nice, as you ought to be. In addition, saying that you don't have the time is often taken as a sign that you don't really take the other person seriously. It will be assumed that you don't respect junior's ambitions to get into television, or your stockbroker friend's musical abilities, or the seriousness of your next-door neighbor's legal problem. Offense will be taken.

In many cases, the best way to avoid being imposed upon is to convince the people who want your expertise that in fact they've come to the wrong source, and then offer an alternative. For example, if someone wants me to advise a son or daughter on how to get into the news business, I tell them that I really don't think I'd be much help. "Things have changed so much since I first started out," I tell them, "that I think it would be a waste of Kathy's time to talk to me." A waste of *Kathy's* time, you'll notice, not mine. Then I add, "There are a couple of very up-to-date books on the subject I'd recommend, though. Some of the younger people around here tell me that they found them very helpful." I give them the titles and conclude by saying that I'd be glad to answer any specific questions Kathy might have after she's read them, but that I doubt if I'll be able to add anything very useful.

In this age of specialization, and of extremely rapid change, almost anybody can get away with suggesting that either somebody else could answer the question or make a judgment better, or that he or she is "out of touch" with what's going on in that particular area of the field these days. If you can suggest someone else for the person to contact, so much the better. That's passing the buck, of course, but there are people who really do like to be asked for their advice, and if you know of someone who won't mind, then there's no harm done. Some people take genuine pleasure in dispensing their expertise. But if you want to *avoid* being imposed on, the best thing you can do is convey the impression that you really don't know it all and wouldn't want to give the other person a bum steer.

Many people not only want free advice, they expect other people to offer their more immediate talents for free. Joe is constantly being asked if he will play the piano at parties. A bachelor friend of mine who happens to be a superb cook tells me that on numerous occasions he's been asked to dinner in the following terms: "If I buy all the ingredients, would you make that wonderful salmon soufflé for our first course?" He says that he sometimes wonders whether he's been invited for his company or to act as caterer. He doesn't mind if he's the only guest and the host or hostess isn't a good cook, but when it's a party for six he begins to think he's being seriously imposed on. Sometimes all people really want is your face or name. Joe and I were once invited to a party on the same evening that we had another engagement. I explained the problem, and the hostess said, "Well, if you could just be here between seven-thirty and eight, it would be a big help. *People* magazine's photographers are going to be here then, and I'd like to have as many celebrities around as possible." As if that weren't bad enough, she went on to say, "We won't really need you after that." Well!

Getting out of these situations can be tricky. My friend the bachelor cook has taken to saying that he really doesn't like to cook in other people's kitchens because the utensils are different, oven temperatures vary, and so on. But he says that that excuse doesn't really go down very well and he generally ends up allowing himself to be imposed upon. The person who's asked to play the piano, sing, or do card tricks at a party is in an even worse position, because the request to perform is usually sprung on them with no advance warning in front of the other guests. One can say that one jammed one's fingers yesterday, or that one has a sore throat. Or one can say, "You know, I'm enjoying myself so much I think I'd rather just sit around and talk."

Whatever you say, however, the host or hostess is going to be put out. That being the case, I think it is sometimes worthwhile to be daring and get to the heart of the matter. The heart of the matter is that you're being asked to do for free what you normally get paid for, or what the hosts would otherwise have to pay someone else to do. Joe was once at a dinner party in a private room of a restaurant. There happened to be a piano in the room, and over coffee Joe was asked to perform. He really wasn't in the mood, but everyone started cajoling him. A friend of his, who was a theatrical agent, said, "Okay, wait a minute. This man is a professional. As of this moment, he's my client." He picked up an empty bread basket and said, "I want five bucks from everybody in this basket." There was a good deal of laughter, some of it rather nervous, everyone coughed up, Joe performed, and the collection was given to the restaurant staff. But a point had been made.

Joe has since been known, on occasion, to say, "Okay, I'll play, but it'll be a buck a song." If you have the kind of personality that allows you to say things like that with a smile and humor in your voice, it's not a bad tactic to use next time someone wants your expertise or your talents for free. You can say, "Sure, but that'll be ten cents a head," Or, "Well, you know, I usually get twenty cents an hour for this kind of thing." You've got to say it lightly, and keep the price absurdly low, but it is an effective way of letting people understand what they're really asking of you.

Maybe next time they won't be so quick to impose.

I Know Your Word Will Make All the Difference

Your neighbor, who moved in late last year, wants you to recommend her for membership in the local country club. A business friend wants his son to go to Yale, and since you're a graduate, who better to write a letter praising junior to the skies. A former employee wants a letter proclaiming what a terrific secretary she is. A friend is looking for a new dentist and wants you to put her in touch with yours.

There are problems. You don't know your new neighbor very well. The business friend's son is an obnoxious little jerk and doesn't seem all that bright. Your former secretary wasn't exactly fired, but you certainly considered it. And your friend has a terror of pain and screams bloody murder even with two shots of novocaine; she's been through five dentists in four years.

When people ask you to recommend them, they are imposing on you twice over. First, they're asking you to take the time and trouble to write the letter or make the phone call. Second, they're asking you to tie your good name to theirs. There's no problem when you think the person is charming, talented, diligent, and an all-round asset to the human race. Curiously, though, people who are all-round assets to the human race seem to require fewer recommendations than people who are having a hard time getting along in the world.

I think refusing to write a letter of recommendation is tantamount to slapping someone across the face, and I almost never say no to such a request. But I'm also extremely careful about what I write or say. I will put up with having my time imposed on, but not my name.

In the four difficult cases described above, what would I say?

About the new neighbor, I could say, "I don't know Mrs. Jones very well, but she seems to be a good mother to her children. She has expressed a desire to join a large number of community clubs and organizations, and her application to the country club is clearly an extension of that eagerness."

About the obnoxious little jerk who wants to go to Yale, I would say, "David seems to have a strong desire to attend Yale, and I'm sure that the stimulus of a first-class college education would be invaluable to him."

About the former secretary, I would say, "Ms. Smith was in my employ for a year and a half. While she did not seem fully at ease in this particular position, I am sure that she is capable of functioning very well in other circumstances."

In the case of the friend with a terror of dentists, though, I would be less evasive. I would call my dentist and say that a friend would be telephoning him for an appointment. I would tell him that she needs a lot of work done, and that he might be just the person for her since he's so good at dealing with people who are afraid of pain.

In the first three instances, I haven't said anything awful. But I have suggested that Mrs. Jones is something of a compulsive "joiner." In the case of David, I have intimated that he needs some stimulus, knowing full well that a college like Yale is looking for self-starters. In terms of the former secretary, it was necessary to get a little more up-front. I don't want anyone hiring an incompetent on my say-so. With my dentist, a fairly overt warning seemed in order.

The nice person may be perfectly willing to be imposed upon in some circumstances, but no one should be required to give away his or her good name for nothing.

5

This Isn't My Job and Other Dodges

Not only do nice people get imposed upon, asked to do countless "small" favors—they are also often asked to take on unfair responsibilities in a larger sense. The difference between an imposition and an unfair responsibility is one of both magnitude and possible repercussions. The imposition may cost you time, effort, or money, and its nuisance value may be high, but the problem is a short-term one. Once the favor is done, the job is behind you. Taking on an unfair responsibility, however, often means allowing yourself to become involved in a situation that is going to bring you not only problems in the present but problems in the future; what's more, the situation is sufficiently complicated that the problems show every sign of getting larger as time passes.

For example, when two friends are on the outs, or a couple is on the verge of splitting up, and one of the people involved comes to you and asks you to talk to the other person for them, you are being asked to take on an unfair responsibility. You're being asked to act as a go-between or a mediator, to become the diplomat who effects a peace treaty. Since you're not Henry Kissinger, it's more than likely that you are not only going to fail at ending the war—you're probably going to end up with both parties mad at you as well as one another.

There's another kind of unfair responsibility that married couples—or live-in lovers, for that matter—often try to impose upon one another. One partner has a friend, whether a new friend or one of long standing, whom they insist that the other partner become friends with, too, regardless of whether or not there is any natural rapport between them. What's more, you're also supposed to become chummy with the friend's spouse or lover. When this means that you're being asked to forge a long-term bond with people you don't much appreciate, you're being requested to take on an unfair responsibility. And it's one that's inevitably going to lead to trouble in the future.

Then there are the unfair responsibilities we fall into by accident, only to suddenly realize that we're trapped in a situation we're sick and tired of. For example, one Thanksgiving you host the gathering of the clan for your various far-flung relatives. Then you do it again the next year, and the next. In the fifth year, you begin to ask yourself, "Why me? Why do I always get stuck with doing all this work?"

I'd like to look at the question of taking on unfair responsibility in three areas, showing how you can:

1. avoid becoming an unwilling mediator;
2. stay out of unwanted relationships;
3. get out of traps you've fallen into.

If Only You'd Talk to Him

Two years ago, an old friend of mine whom I'll call Jim split up with the woman he'd been living with for three years. I'd grown very fond of Gail, too, over that period of time, and I was sorry to see it happen. But what can you do? These things occur all the time.

Gail, however, thought there was something I could do. Jim had walked out on her, rather than the other way around, and she was devastated by it. She still loved Jim, and was convinced that he still loved her in spite of everything. Gail took me to lunch and begged me to go to Jim and plead her case for her.

As she talked, a dozen reasons why I didn't want to, and shouldn't, act as Gail's emissary raced through my head. First of all, I knew that Jim had become involved with another woman, and that that was probably the main reason why he'd left Gail. How much Gail knew about that relationship I wasn't certain. From the way she was talking, she probably didn't know much or refused to take it seriously. From my point of view, though, she was not only asking me to patch things up between herself and Jim, but also, in effect, to tell Jim to break off his new relationship. That's dangerous territory. You simply don't tell people whom they really ought to be in love with.

Then there was the fact that Jim had been a friend of mine for a very long time, going way back before he'd even known Gail. That was one reason why Gail thought I could lay it on the line to Jim. It was also a major reason why I didn't want to talk to him. He would feel pressured, resent the intrusion and, quite naturally, assume that I was taking Gail's side. The fact that he and I had been friends for so long would lead him to feel that I had betrayed him. I didn't want that to happen. Ideally, I would have liked to remain friends with both Jim and Gail, but if that couldn't be, Jim came first in my affections. What's more, if I went to Jim and failed to persuade him to have a go at working things out with Gail, she would think I hadn't tried as hard as I could have, and for exactly the reason why she'd selected me as mediator in the first place: the fact that Jim and I were so close.

It's called Catch-22, and it always crops up in these situations.

There's a fundamental rule that applies here. Don't get into mediation unless you're 100 percent sure you can patch things up. Not 99 percent sure, 100 percent. Otherwise, you're going to find yourself becoming sandwiched between two angry people. And it's more than likely that *you're* the one who will end up as chopped liver.

In refusing to act as a mediator, I think that the nicest and most sensible thing to do is be utterly frank. This is not the time for white lies. What I said to Gail was this: "You know how fond I am of both of you, and I'm sorry there are problems. But I know Jim well enough to realize that he'd resent my talking to him. He'd feel I was intruding. And he'd also be angry at you for asking me to talk to him. It would make things worse, not better."

Gail replied, "But you don't have to tell him I asked you."

This was a response I was expecting. The mediator is always supposed to pretend that the whole thing is his or her idea.

"Look, Gail," I said, "I can't say the things to Jim that you want me to say without giving the game away. He'll know that I've talked to you, and he'll assume that you asked me to go to him. He's not going to believe it's all my idea. He'll ask me, and I really can't lie about it."

When someone asks you to be a mediator, you are inevitably going to find yourself put in the position of having to tell only part of the truth to both sides. You're being asked to manipulate a situation that isn't of your own making. And that's an unfair responsibility.

Don't do it. Don't take on that responsibility. It will only get you into trouble with at least one and probably both of the parties to the dispute. Whenever you are asked to be a mediator, imagine a big rubber mallet poised over your head. Because if you accept the responsibility, you're going to get hit with that figurative mallet.

Be frank in explaining why you can't offer your assistance if it's at all possible. But whatever you give by way of excuse, get out of it.

You Don't Have to See a Lot of Them

A couple of years after we were married, Joe began cultivating the friendship of a man I'll call Brian, largely for business reasons. And Joe kept trying to get me into the picture. "Why don't we have Brian and his wife over to dinner," he'd say. Or, "Why don't we all have a night on the town."

From my point of view, there were good reasons why not. Brian was an amiable man, and his wife Claire seemed quite sweet. But I didn't find either of them very interesting, and I didn't want to get involved in endless social Ping-Pong with them. I'd met them casually at parties and I wanted to keep it that way. For one thing, Claire was one of those women with nothing to do and a lot of money to spend, and I knew that if the relationship got beyond being casual, she'd be calling me up all the time suggesting we have lunch together or go on shopping sprees or asking if she could come along with me to a film screening. No thank you. I had neither the time nor the inclination to become one of Claire's "buddies."

Joe didn't understand my reluctance. We wouldn't have to see all that much of Brian and Claire, he argued, and it would be a help to him. Sure it would—Joe found Brian fairly boring, too. But, in the long run, I thought I'd do Joe more harm than good. I explained to him that if I got involved, Claire would inevitably be after me to do things with her all the time, that often I would have to say no, and that since I really wasn't much interested in Claire as a person, I'd have to be acting a role that wasn't very comfortable. People can tell when you're not a sincere, full-fledged friend, and I could just hear Claire saying to her husband, "You know, I'm not sure Pat really likes me all that much," or, worse, "I really think Pat's kind of a snob." And what would that do to Joe's relationship with Brian?

I suggested to Joe that he should cultivate his friendship and business relationship with Brian as much on his own as possible, having lunch, taking him to a Knicks game, or whatever. Occasionally, when I had a screening or a Broadway opening to attend, maybe all four of us could meet for an early evening drink, and then he could take Brian and Claire to dinner afterward while I went about my work.

And that was the way we did it.

In my view, nice people do not have the obligation to become friends with every last person a spouse or live-in lover happens to like. It just isn't realistic. When two people get married or decide to live together, they each bring along the furniture of their lives, actual sofas and paintings and kitchen utensils as well as the friends they have made over the years. And it is almost always true that there isn't room for everything. Some of the furniture goes in the cellar or is given away, and some of the friends fall by the wayside, by mutual agreement. Where there isn't a mutual agreement, in the case of friends, I see nothing wrong with each individual seeing some people separately. In fact, I think it's essential. Otherwise, you're asking your spouse to pretend to be good friends with someone he or she doesn't much care about—and that's an unfair responsibility.

And the same goes for new people you meet along the way. The concept of the couple as Siamese twins doesn't work in today's world; seeing some people separately is a much better solution than forcing one partner to become involved in relationships he or she would rather avoid.

This doesn't mean ostracizing your partner's solo friends altogether, of course. One can join up for a drink occasionally, as I did with Brian and Claire. Or, one partner may have friends over to watch a football game or play cards, with the other partner putting in an appearance briefly and saying hello, but not actively joining in.

As I've said before, even the nicest person has only so much patience, only so much energy and time, only so much to give. It's pointless and eventually self-defeating to use up your patience and energy by taking on the unfair responsibility of being extra nice to people you don't really care about. Plain polite is enough.

How Did I Get Myself into This?

All of us have had the experience of doing something nice for other people, only to discover that we're expected to keep doing it over and over again. Take that Thanksgiving feast you've been preparing for your relatives and their assorted spouses for the past five years. Last year, there were fourteen people, at two tables, and everyone had a wonderful time—except you. It took you three days of advance work to prepare the meal, and another two days to get your house fully in order again afterward. On the holiday itself you felt like a stranger at your own party because you were never in the living room or dining room long enough to figure out the flow of the conversation. Oh, sure, some people asked if they could help, but that offer, in practical terms, meant could they get in the way. The one person who really wanted to be in the kitchen was your Aunt Martha, who kept saying things like, "Don't you think you should baste the turkey more often, dear?"

Afterward, you said to yourself, "Never again." You got yourself into this by being a nice person; can you also get yourself out of it nicely?

What's happened is that a pattern has been established. And it's got to be broken. But you can't simply announce that you're not going to give a Thanksgiving party this year. For one thing, there's no way you can get out of spending Thanksgiving with your mother and your husband's father. They'd be terribly hurt, and in fact you have a sentimental attachment to being with them on that day yourself. But if you have just them, everybody who's been disinvited is going to be furious.

But there are other ways to break the pattern less drastically and still unload some of the unfair responsibility you've taken on. In this particular situation, you might, for example, suggest that it could be fun to experiment a little this year, and try a potluck Thanksgiving with everybody bringing a favorite dish. Yes, everyone has always brought something in the past—nuts, candy, fruit, wine, the occasional mince pie. But what you want is to get out of the kitchen. The trouble with this means of breaking the pattern is that there are going to be some people who say, "Oh, but you're a so much better cook than I am." If that happens to be true, you're still trapped.

There's an alternative, though, which will thoroughly break the pattern. You say, "We've decided that we're going to have Thanksgiving at a restaurant this year as a special treat. I'm going to take care of all the organizing. We can get a special price of twenty-five dollars a person if we pay in advance, so if you want to join in you can just send me a check and I'll arrange everything for us." This alternative takes a little more nerve, of course. For that reason, it's a good idea to enlist an accomplice who's willing to say that the whole thing is "really my idea." Among that passel of relatives there's bound to be someone you can be frank with and explain that Thanksgiving has gotten out of hand and that you need a break. Enlisting an accomplice will take a lot of the heat off you, while the fact that you're doing the organizing will help to allay the impression that you're shirking your expected holiday responsibility. Some of your relatives are going to be annoyed, there's no way around it. They've been getting their turkey for free and suddenly they're expected to cough up twenty-five dollars a head. But the people who are annoyed are likely to be the same ones whose company you could most happily do without, the same ones who are impervious to the thought that they've been loading you down with an unfair responsibility. Forcing them to pay may mean that they won't come, but, annoyed though they may be, it's *their* decision. They have been invited to take part. They'd be a lot angrier if you gave the dinner at your home as usual and didn't invite them.

The important point is that you've broken the pattern. You've deflated the *assumption* that you're going to go on endlessly doing what other people expect of you. That means that you are once again a free person.

I don't think it's possible to unload an unfair responsibility, of whatever kind, that you've been shouldering for some time without creating some temporary hard feelings. But if you can break the pattern with some finesse by altering the kind or degree of the responsibility you're willing to accept, nobody's going to stay mad for too long. And even if they do, that's better than suffering silently while your inner anger mounts. Because eventually that anger will find expression—you'll finally blow up and say to people in so many words that they've been taking advantage of you. And that can end in an ugly scene.

The nice person doesn't have an obligation to assume unfair responsibilities in the first place. But if you get trapped, it's going to be better for everyone involved if you change the pattern before you explode. Nice people do explode sometimes, and they often have a right to do so. But the nice person also realizes that it's better to disappoint than to lose himself or herself to anger.

6

Taking Sides and Coming to the Rescue

The nice person is often well advised to stay out of other people's problems. It's really none of your business that the couple next door or in the apartment above you were yelling at one another last night, and if you start asking questions of either half of the couple, you're just being nosey. If someone asks you to mediate a dispute he or she is having with a friend or a spouse, you're probably being asked to take on an unfair responsibility; you'll be seen as taking sides, and may only make things worse. But sometimes it's important, and the only nice thing to do is to take sides and come to the rescue of someone who's being treated unfairly or badly.

In trying to determine when to come to the rescue, we have to make some clear distinctions between butting in and offering constructive help. As always, it's a matter of looking at the context, the who, what, where, and when of it. When considering whether or not to take sides or come to the rescue, there are four questions we need to ask ourselves:

Am I helping or interfering?
Am I doing it for the other person or myself?
Can I really make the situation better?
Am I willing to accept the consequences of my actions?

Sometimes the line between helping and interfering is very clear-cut. When your mother-in-law starts telling you how to raise your kids, she's interfering and she ought not to be doing it. If you tell your best friend that her husband (or his wife) is probably cheating on her (or him), you're certainly not helping; your friend may already know what's going on and hasn't brought it up with you because she or he doesn't want to discuss it—or your friend may very much *not* want to know what's going on. Either way, you're butting in.

On other occasions, though, things may be a lot more confusing, and the line between helping and interfering hard to draw. In fact, there are times when in order to help we have to interfere. If you have become aware that a friend of one of your kids is a victim of child abuse, it certainly ought to be reported to the appropriate social agency. That's definitely interfering in other people's lives, but the gravity of the situation fully justifies doing so. The context requires action.

Asking yourself whether the action you're contemplating is for your sake or the other person's helps to clarify the matter further, and acts as a check on the tendency to interfere without sufficient cause. If you're doing it primarily for yourself, forget it. Sometimes, however, you may be doing it both for yourself *and* the other person. For example, if you're giving a dinner party and one of your guests starts attacking his or her spouse in front of everyone, you might want to take sides not only to rescue the beleaguered spouse but also because the scene is embarrassing your other guests and spoiling the party.

The third question, as to whether you can really make the situation any better, is a crucial one. Unless you have a good chance of succeeding at changing the situation, it's usually wiser not to try. That's because it's almost axiomatic that if you don't improve things you will only make them worse.

Finally, you have to be willing to accept the consequences of your actions. You have to ask yourself if you're going to be able to live with the possibility that your offer of help may be spurned, or that one of the people involved may become angry with you. If you can't accept the possibility of unhappy results, then it's best to stay out of it.

I'd like to examine how and when the nice person should take sides or come to the rescue in several areas:

1. taking sides in petty quarrels;
2. standing up for and standing by friends;
3. telling people they need help.

A Bridge over Troubled Waters

As a general rule, it could be said that the more petty the quarrel, the wiser the nice person is to stay out of it. But even a petty argument can end with someone in tears, or become so uncomfortable to those witnessing it that the nice person has to step in and try to act as a bridge over the churning waters.

A friend related a story to me that is a perfect example of how a very silly argument can escalate into a potentially awful situation—one that requires the nice person to take action. During the 1981 baseball playoffs, Jim had three friends over to eat pasta and watch the first game between the Yankees and Kansas City. One friend was Libby, a divorced woman whom Jim had known since college days. Bart and Kathy, who had moved to New York four years earlier and lived in Jim's apartment building, completed the foursome.

I should state right off that I personally find nothing more ridiculous than people getting into heated arguments over sports teams or the strengths and deficiencies of individual players, but I'm also aware that that is part of the American way of life and goes on in stadiums, bars, and living rooms across the land every day and night of the year. And that's exactly what happened at Jim's on this particular October night. Jim and Libby had both grown up in Massachusetts and were Red Sox fans from childhood. All Red Sox fans, as I know from my own experience of growing up in Massachusetts, despise and loathe the Yankees. So, of course, Jim and Libby were rooting for Kansas City to win the playoffs and move on to the World Series. Bart and Kathy, however, as recent citizens of New York, had taken up the Yankee cause with the fervor of the newly converted. As Jim says, "I should have known there would be trouble."

Libby happened to be the most knowledgeable and hard-core baseball fan present; Kathy was the least informed. Jim and Libby, exhibiting their old Red Sox colors, put down the Yankees at every turn. But what started out in a good-natured way began to turn ugly. Libby began deriding not just the Yankees, but Kathy's knowledge of the game, implying and finally actually saying that if Kathy knew anything at all about baseball, she couldn't possibly root for the Yankees. It occurred to Jim that there was a "subplot" to this argument—perhaps based on the fact that Kathy was both considerably younger than Libby and extremely attractive.

By this time, Jim had dropped out of the dialogue, since Kathy seemed to be getting upset. Kathy's husband Bart was egging Libby on, but instead of attacking him, Libby kept coming back at the more vulnerable Kathy. Finally, Jim, despite his long friendship with Libby and the fact that he basically agreed with her about the Yankees, saw that he was going to have to stop what was going on. He was sitting next to Libby and he said to her, quietly, "Don't you think we should let up a little?"

Libby replied loudly, "Why should we let up? I don't see why people should be allowed to get away with being plain stupid."

At this point Jim decided that he had to take sides, firmly. He said to Kathy, "Just ignore Libby." And to Libby he said, "All right, stop it."

But he was too late. Kathy got up and ran to the bathroom in tears, As for Libby, she didn't speak to Jim for half an hour and was extremely cool for the rest of the evening, despite the fact that Kathy came back in a calmer state and Libby made no more comments that weren't strictly focused on the game that was unfolding on television.

Jim says that he should have stepped in sooner, should have said enough already, and taken sides, before things got so far out of hand. He adds, "The problem was that I agreed with a lot of Libby's points. And that kept me from realizing until too late how nasty and personal she was being about making them. I didn't put a stop to things soon enough. And it was my job. I was the host."

In saying that, Jim is recognizing the importance of both context and territory. And when he told Libby to stop it, and took sides with Kathy, he says he was fully aware that Libby would be angry with him. He was willing to take the consequences.

Taking sides in an argument of this kind isn't easy, but there are times when the nice person has got to take on the burden of doing it.

Taking Up the Cudgels

I am standing with a small group of women at a neighborhood party. One woman says she's been reading excerpts from Helen Gurley Brown's book, *Having It All,* in the *New York Post.* "It's really embarrassing," she says. "How an older married woman can write about one-night stands and extramarital sex that way is just beyond me."

"It's really kind of disgusting," another woman comments.

Idle chatter. But it so happens that both Helen Gurley Brown and her movie-producer husband David Brown are friends of Joe's and mine. Shall I just let these comments pass, or shall I come to Helen's defense? Actually, I've been in this situation before. Helen is a highly visible and certainly controversial figure, and since knocking people with power is such an easy and gratifying activity, Helen gets a good deal of flak. I myself am sometimes taken aback by Helen's public frankness about sex, but I also like and respect her very much.

If you are a true pal, or even a good acquaintance, of someone who's being knocked behind his or her back, I believe the nice person has an obligation to come to the rescue. Besides, if my neighbor is so shocked, how come she's had her nose buried in the *Post* in the first place?

"Actually," I say, "I know Helen quite well, and she's a very nice, savvy lady. What's more, she knows her readership down to their toes. It may not be what you or I want to read about, but in terms of her audience it's obviously right on target. That's why she's so successful."

When the nice person is defending a friend or acquaintance, it's important to do it in such a way that it doesn't seem like an attack on the person who's doing the criticizing. Telling people that they don't know what they're talking about is to be strenuously avoided. What you want to do instead is to indicate that you understand what they're talking about, but that there's more to the person you're defending than just the aspect that's being criticized.

For example, suppose your friend Marianne is being knocked because she's always such a squeaky wheel at PTA meetings, asking questions and demanding attention. You could reply, "I know she seems a little pushy, but it's because she's such a concerned mother. And you have to admit she does get action."

And then there's Stan, the silent one in your car pool. Someone's running him down for being a total bore. Your comeback might be, "Well, he doesn't say much, but there's another side to him. When you get onto the subject of something he really knows about, he's a very articulate guy."

Your friend Larry makes $200,000 a year, but people are always saying he isn't very bright and wouldn't have gotten anywhere if it weren't for his father-in-law. You might say, "Yes, a lot of people say that about Larry. But I wouldn't underestimate him. He's got a lot of responsibility and the old man isn't the type to jeopardize company profits for anyone."

Things can get a lot more complicated, however, if you're trying to defend a friend who is in some kind of trouble. For instance, a film producer I've known for a long time was the subject of a great many rumors a couple of years ago. A former associate of his had been indicted for embezzlement, and my friend Peter's name kept coming up at the trial even though he hadn't been charged with any wrongdoing. A lot of Peter's supposed friends decided to put as much distance as possible between themselves and him. Who could tell, maybe he might get indicted yet? Suddenly Peter and his wife weren't getting invited to a great many parties whose guest lists they would have headed a few months before.

Well, we all know about rats and sinking ships. In our

society, even a whiff of real trouble causes a great many not very nice people to drop a friend overnight. You don't have to have done anything wrong—mere suspicion is enough.

In Peter's case a lot of people began asking me questions about "how he was taking it," with veiled suggestions that he might end up behind bars any minute. My reply was, "Well, I know there are a lot of rumors flying around, but Peter seems to be completely ignoring them. He certainly doesn't seem at all concerned."

One day I went into a restaurant in the theater district to have a business lunch with a well-known publicist. As I was being shown to his table, I spotted Peter, lunching at another table, and I went over to say hello. I gave him a peck on the cheek and we chatted briefly. When I got to my table, the publicist, who also knew Peter, although not well, said, "Aren't you being a little cozy with Peter So-and-So under the circumstances?"

"Not at all," I said, "he's a friend."

"Good for you," said the publicist.

Well, maybe, but I think it's too bad that we live in a world in which one gets credit for standing by or sticking up for friends. I always thought that was what nice people did as a matter of course.

You Need Help

Some people are excessively free with their advice. Instant experts all, they always know what's best for you. They tell you that you really ought to go on a diet, stop smoking, take up jogging, go to their doctor or dentist or lawyer, join this club, take that job, buy such and such a car, or you're going to ruin your life! This isn't really free advice, it's coercion, and I don't think nice people ought to be charging around telling other people how to run their lives. Most of us have enough difficulty running our own lives, if we stop to think about it, and our energies would be better used solving our own problems.

But there are exceptions. Sometimes people really do need help. Because of force of circumstance, or fear, or because of psychological problems, they have reached the point where they are unable to help themselves or face up to the fact that they *need* help—usually professional help. The alcoholic, the battered wife, the victim of "burn-out," the potential suicide—people in desperate situations. Few of us can get through life without having to deal with a close friend or relative who simply has to be told: you need help.

As a nice person you will come to the rescue. You will lay it on the line to them, tell them again and again why they need help, bully them if necessary, make appointments for them with doctors, psychiatrists, or social workers—appointments which they may fail to keep, forcing you to try again. You will hold them when they break down in sobs, and keep your temper when they lash out at you because they do not want to hear what you are saying.

Aside from coping with the death of a loved one or going through a divorce, nothing is more traumatic than the process of forcing someone to save himself or herself, of making them seek the help they need. Such situations are highly individualistic and it is impossible to recommend any one approach. But there are several things that should be kept in mind when it becomes apparent that someone is in such serious straits.

Don't come to the rescue unless you're feeling strong yourself. The weak can't lead the weak.

Don't come to the rescue expecting to be thanked. You may be thanked later, and profusely, but at the start your attempt to help may be seriously resented.

Don't come to the rescue without recognizing that you may fail.

Don't blame yourself if you do fail.

Don't try to analyze the person's problem for them. Your job isn't to play doctor or psychiatrist, it's simply to get the person to the real thing.

Finally, and most important, don't expect your relationship with the person ever to be the same again. As a result of your efforts, the relationship may grow and eventually be enriched. But things may also go the other way, even if you succeed in forcing the person to get help. You won't be saving what used to be; you can only hope to create what is to be.

Whenever you take sides, or come to the rescue, you are inevitably dealing a new hand of cards.

7

Changing Friendships, or "That's a Wrap"

Friendships come in all shapes and sizes, from mere acquaintanceship to lifelong intimacy. Friendships also change. In college, you may have been very close to Susan and been little more than an acquaintance of Bob's. Ten years later, it's quite possible to have lost touch with Susan but to have formed a real bond with Bob. Friendships change because people change and circumstances change. And sometimes those changes can be difficult to deal with.

The nice person is likely to have a lot of friends—even too many friends. As a nice person, you may be too trusting, developing relationships with people who like you only so long as you agree with them. At the other end of the scale you may find yourself involved in friendships that are too close, that place too many demands upon you. The nice person may try too hard and too long to maintain a friendship that is undergoing a natural process of dissolution. And the nice person may have a very difficult time ending a friendship that has outlived its pleasures or its usefulness in the fullest sense of the word.

The easiest and perhaps ultimately the most gratifying friendships are the "old shoes" relationships formed when you were a child or at college or working at your first job. You may not see one another very often, live in different cities, keep in touch only casually, and yet when you do see one another you can pick up again as though it were yesterday. The most difficult friendships are with people who care so much that they want and expect you to put them ahead of all other friends, and who as a result become overly possessive or even plain jealous.

The friendships we form as kids or at college usually have a certain purity to them. Two individuals just plain like one another. When we're adults, things become more complicated, and we sometimes form friendships because they are convenient, useful, or even necessary relationships. You do like these people, of course, but if it weren't for the fact that you work with them, or live next door, or have kids in the same class at school, the friendships might not have developed to the extent they did. Then things change. You take a different job, or they do, or you move across town or to a different part of the country, you've taken different forks in the road or your goals have altered, and you discover that the basis for the relationship doesn't exist anymore. That's no problem if both people involved recognize that fact, but it often happens that one or the other wants to keep the friendship alive out of its natural environment. That can lead to problems for the nice person who knows that the friendship isn't really viable anymore but doesn't want to hurt the other person's feelings.

There are two changes in circumstance that undoubtedly affect more friendships than any others: getting married and getting divorced. Even very close and long-lasting friendships can founder in either case. Your close friend Sandy can't stand the man or woman you're marrying—or vice versa. Or

Joan and Howard have had a very bitter divorce and insist that you choose between them. In either situation, it means the end of a friendship. How does the nice person go about that guilt-inducing necessity?

Let's look at how the nice person can cope with changing friendships in several areas:

1. The "look at it my way" friendship
2. The overly demanding friendship
3. The altered friendship
4. Ending a friendship

As Long As You Agree with Me

In the mid-1970s Joe got taken up in a big way by a group of men who were "heavy hitters" in New York City political and financial circles. He was being invited hither and yon to important parties and events of the sort that get written up in the newspapers because they're where "the real business of New York" is conducted. Joe thought he'd acquired a whole new set of friends, people who valued his talent, his company, and his opinion. But as it turned out, they didn't want any opinions that didn't agree with theirs.

Very early in the 1976 presidential campaign, Joe decided on his candidate: an obscure former Georgia governor named Jimmy Carter. That choice did not sit at all well with Joe's new friends, who were backing Mo Udall, the liberal Arizona representative. They derided Jimmy Carter and tried to make Joe see the error of his ways. And when he wouldn't back off or change his mind, many of them dropped him completely from their guest lists.

Joe was both annoyed and hurt. But he was not about to throw aside his own convictions in order to "stay in" with these people. In fact, Joe did a lot of work for the Carter campaign, got to know the future president personally, and developed a lasting friendship with his press secretary, Jody Powell. And, lo and behold, after Jimmy Carter's election, the people who had dropped Joe several months before suddenly began cultivating him again. After all, Joe now had "White House connections." Joe's initial temptation was to tell them where to go and what to do with their "friendship." But it was my feeling that he should go along with being cultivated once again, not forgetting to ask these "friends" from time to time, tongue in cheek, what their own candidate was now doing. A nice person, in my view, has a right to take a little discreet revenge and to savor the pleasures of being in the catbird seat.

There is a postscript to this story that helps to define the difference between true friends and "so long as you agree with me" friends even more clearly. In 1982, Joe was asked to write a song ("To Love a Child") to be recorded by Frank Sinatra, which would celebrate First Lady Nancy Reagan's pet project, the "Foster Grandparents" program. Having supported Jimmy Carter just as strongly in 1980 as he had in 1976, Joe was hesitant, but he has always felt that the well-being of children is a non-partisan issue and that the power of the White House can help any worthwhile cause, so he agreed to do it. He then discovered that there was to be a highly publicized White House ceremony, involving Mr. Sinatra, a chorus of children, and the Marines (that is, the Marine Band) to unveil the song and Nancy Reagan's book on the program. As composer, Joe was naturally an honored guest. That honor concerned him; he was particularly worried that our good friend Jody Powell would see it as a kind of betrayal. In fact, Jody was wonderful about it and invited Joe and me to have dinner with himself and his wife, Nan, the night before the ceremony. Jody is a sensitive, witty, and amusing man, and he did have considerable fun with Joe on the subject, but he made it very clear that it wouldn't affect their friendship in the slightest. Besides, he said, it was always good to have a "mole" in the White House, even if it was only for an afternoon . . . and he was only a songwriter at that.

Nice people do not require their friends to agree with them all the time. Nor do nice people try to regulate a friend's relationships with other people, even when they have a valid reason to disapprove.

The nice person who finds that a supposed friend demands agreement or is attempting to regulate his or her associations should be very wary. Fortunately, "as long as you agree with me" friends tend to give themselves away at every turn. They say things like, *"I can't believe* you voted for so-and-so." Or, *"How could you have* liked that movie." Or, *"How can you stand* so-and-so." Or, *"You don't really mean that."* All these phrases are put-downs, and strong indicators that you'd better agree—or else. When a supposed friend talks to you in such terms, I think it's time to back away from the relationship. Because if you don't knuckle under, you're going to get dumped, or find yourself arguing constantly. Either way, the game isn't worth the effort. Nice people generally have better things to do.

Too Close for Comfort

Lord Byron wrote, "Friendship is love without his wings." There is, I believe, a great deal of psychological truth packed into that line of poetry. Close friends make an emotional investment in one another that is very much akin to love; the feelings they have about one another partake of love's profound caring and concern, but also of love's jealousy and possessiveness. But the wings—the sexual enthrallment—are missing. When lovers quarrel, the beating of those wings can save them. A caress, a kiss, and the tempest is past. When friends quarrel, it can be more difficult to patch things up.

Nice people can come to expect too much of one another in a close friendship. Rituals of togetherness often develop which can ultimately create problems. Whether it's a tradition of sharing certain holidays, a regular Friday night poker session, buying season tickets together to basketball games or the opera, renting a summer cottage together, or even making a weekly trip to a shopping center, such rituals become entrenched to the point that if either individual (or couple) wants to change the pattern, the other individual or couple is likely to feel hurt.

If, for instance, two couples have rented a seaside cottage together for a couple of weeks every summer for four years, and one couple decides that they want to do something different the fifth year, whether it's drive to the Grand Canyon or take a trip to Europe, the other couple is going to feel bereft. If they can't afford the seaside cottage on their own, they're also going to be angry. If they are angry or hurt and let it show, the couple who's changing the pattern may feel guilty—and at the same time resent the fact that they feel that way. If, in fact, they wanted to do something different last year but held off because they didn't want to disappoint their friends, they may become angry in turn.

The bereft couple may be so eager to maintain the ritual in substance if not in form that they'll say, "Oh, what a wonderful idea. It is time we did something different. We've always wanted to see the Grand Canyon ourselves. Why don't we make it a foursome?"

The reason why not, of course, is that the couple breaking the pattern is probably doing it on purpose. It's not going to the seaside that they want to avoid, but rather the perpetual foursome. It's not that they don't continue to care about their friends—it's just that the ritual has gotten to be a responsibility, something they *have* to participate in whether they really want to or not. When friends become too close for comfort, and a sense of claustrophobia begins to develop on either side, the potential for trouble is high.

I think it is one of the tasks of the nice person to be alert to the possibility that a claustrophobic ritual is developing, and to do something about it before it gets out of hand. You'll be doing yourself a favor and ensuring a healthier, more relaxed friendship at the same time. Ritual togetherness has a way of creeping up on us, unfortunately. You have to be on your guard. For example, if you spend New Year's Eve with the same couple two years in a row, I'd make it a point to do something else the third year. Changing the pattern at that point won't cause any bad feelings. But if the pattern gets established to the point that you find yourself saying, "Oh, we *always* spend New Year's Eve with the Smiths," you're in trouble. Never let yourself get into an "always" situation with friends, no matter how close they are. "Always" is a very restrictive word, and when you start feeling restricted you're going to wish you could get back to saying "sometimes." But by then it's going to be difficult to do that without causing bad feelings all around.

In fact, I think it's wise to keep things on a "sometimes" basis in all areas of social intercourse. I try very hard, for instance, to avoid getting trapped into playing what I call social Ping-Pong. You have the Joneses for dinner, and then they invite you, and then you invite them—no, please. That's getting into an obligatory situation and a boring one to boot. The nice person shouldn't feel obliged to be constantly giving tit for tat, and shouldn't expect other nice people to do it either. That can lead to ritual, and with ritual a sense of obligation and/or expectation that is bound to create hard feelings on one side or the other in the long run.

Forks in the Road

Before her marriage to Governor John Y. Brown of Kentucky, Phyllis George and I saw a great deal of one another. She and Joe got along famously and our kids adored her. We're still good friends today, but the nature of the friendship inevitably underwent a change. To a large extent this was simply a matter of geography. In our extremely mobile society, most of us have discovered that a friendship, no matter how close, is not quite the same when one person moves a thousand miles away—or for that matter, even one hundred miles away. One can try to bridge the gap with telephone calls, letters, and "getting together" when the person who has moved away comes to town, but a certain casual connectedness is always lost. In addition, both friends will meet new people or develop new interests that can no longer be shared with one another as they occur. There is thus bound to be, on both sides, a sense of having lost touch to some degree.

Phyllis tried to bridge the geography gap by inviting Joe and me to Kentucky. But because both Joe and I travel so much and have so many commitments to fulfill, we had to decline several times. I think that Phyllis was somewhat hurt, that she felt perhaps we didn't want to come—which was not the case—or that we weren't doing our part to maintain the friendship. For my part, I felt at times a little guilty that we couldn't, in fact, fly down to Kentucky at the drop of a hat.

When the hurt feelings on one side, or the guilt on the other, get out of hand in situations like this, it can mean that the friendship is effectively over. But if both friends understand that a change in the nature of the friendship is inevitably going to be effected by the sheer geographical distance that now exists, it is possible to make the transition to a new kind of friendship, less intimate, usually, but still motivated by mutual fondness and respect. Fortunately, that was what happened with Phyllis. She still sends presents to the kids on their birthdays and at Christmas, we keep in touch as best we can, and see one another when we can. Because we both travel a lot, there is always the chance of having the unexpected pleasure of running into one another by surprise at some far-flung event. Our friendship, in a different form, endures.

With the understanding that it is bound to be different, friendship can triumph over geographic separation. It is often more difficult, however, to preserve a friendship when one friend suddenly achieves a status, fame, or financial success denied to the other. Take the example of Sheila and Carole. Both women are suburban housewives in their late thirties, and have been friends since junior high school. Their friendship has always been marked by a certain good-natured competitiveness—who could get the best buy on an oriental rug, who raised the best roses, who could give the most elegant dinner party, that kind of thing. Their husbands were both successful businessmen, earning perhaps $100,000 a year. But then, suddenly, the specalized electronics company owned by Sheila's husband was bought out by a large corporation, and he found himself richer by many millions of dollars. Sheila and her husband embarked on an entirely new life-style—diamonds and sables and yachts and a mansion to live in. Sheila can now have just about anything she wants, and Carole cannot even begin to compete. Since their relationship was based on friendly competitiveness, its roots have been destroyed.

I know both these women, and I've watched their friendship unravel. Sheila, unfortunately, has taken to being rich in the worst possible way, flaunting her fur coats and jewels in every direction, most especially in Carole's direction. That's not a nice thing to do, of course, and it's driving Carole crazy. She has become increasingly envious and resentful; her husband is just plain angry at Sheila's behavior and what it's doing to his wife. It's clear that unless Sheila drastically changes her ways, she's not going to have Carole around to impress much longer.

I've seen success destroy a lot of friendships. It's always hardest to deal with when the two friends are in the same field, when one writer makes the best-seller list while his pal is still struggling to pay the rent, when one lawyer gets elected to Congress while his old friend is still drawing up wills, when one model gets on the cover of *Vogue* while her roommate considers herself lucky to get a job doing a commercial for a local furniture store. Suddenly, the two friends have become "unequal." They're no longer peers. That can be especially galling if the person who's left behind, as it were, is actually the more talented of the two, and the other achieved his or her success by sheer drive or, worse still, dumb luck.

If the less successful person is very self-confident and feels that his or her turn will come, the friendship may not be greatly affected. But even if that's the case, the major responsibility for maintaining the friendship rests with the person who's moved up in the world. The nice person will avoid crowing, avoid flaunting the trappings of success, and above all avoid running off at the mouth about all the wonderful things that are happening in his or her life. That doesn't mean that the newly successful person has to pretend that *nothing's* really happened—it just means waiting to be asked questions instead of *announcing* the good news; in this case it does not pay to advertise. The nice person—indeed the smart person—will also keep in mind the fact that what goes up can and often does come down. A little humility is always a good thing; in situations of this sort it's a necessity.

On the other side of the coin, nice people ought to be able to take at least some pleasure in a friend's success. After all, the fact that a good friend has triumphed says something about your worth too. You have been, and are, a friend of a person who's achieved a lot. There wouldn't have been a friendship in the first place if that person didn't respect your abilities and value your judgment and emotional support. That doesn't mean you shouldn't feel the occasional twinge of jealousy or envy, which is only natural. But because success often brings greater pressures as well as pleasures, your emotional support may prove as valuable, or even more valuable than ever, if you don't let your envy become so intense that it makes your friend feel uncomfortable. While the major responsibility for being nice in these circumstances rests with the newly successful friend, it also needs to be reciprocated.

Of course, if you're dealing with a Sheila, who had nothing to do with earning her sudden wealth and has the bad taste and lack of discretion to use it as a social weapon, the time has come to recognize that your old friend isn't a very nice person after all. And, sad though it may be, it's time to end the relationship.

That's a Wrap

In television, when a taping session ends, we say, "That's a wrap." Sometimes we have to say that about a friendship. Because it's simply over.

Ending a friendship is painful. But it is something that we all have to do from time to time.

Before I met Joe, in the days when I was working as a reporter for NBC's "Channel 4 News" in New York, I became friends with the wife of a well-known writer. I'll call her Kate. She was a very intelligent person, but she was also high-strung, the kind of person who always thinks there's something going on she doesn't know about, and who therefore wants to get everything under control. For instance, she was always accusing her husband of having affairs with other women, even though he wasn't. In the end, he did have an affair, on the grounds that if he was going to suffer the accusations, he might as well enjoy the pleasures of an extramarital fling. The marriage eventually collapsed, and after Kate had separated from her husband, she began putting a lot of her energy into organizing *my* life, including telling me whom I should be friends with.

Although I was fond of Kate and very close to her children, I didn't much appreciate her attempts to run my life. Matters came to a head after I became engaged to Joe. Kate didn't like Joe and did everything in the book to discourage our relationship. She let him know very clearly that she didn't like him, and kept telling me stories about him. They weren't nice stories, and while I didn't confront Joe with them, there were cases where it was possible to check them out by talking to other people. It turned out that the stories weren't true. Kate persisted in running Joe down, and it became clear that I had to make a choice between Kate and Joe—I couldn't have both people in my life. My choice was obviously going to be Joe, which meant that I had to end my friendship with Kate.

I did it badly.

When she left messages for me, I simply didn't return the calls; when she got through to me personally, I said I was too busy to see her, or had another engagement. I was cold and distant, and eventually she stopped calling.

I felt guilty about the way I'd handled the situation, especially in respect to Kate's children. I'd spent a lot of time with them while Kate was going through the trauma of her divorce, and I knew they weren't going to understand why I had suddenly dropped so completely out of their lives.

But I did learn some lessons.

The ending of a friendship is one circumstance in which

I think the nice person simply has to summon up the guts to face the issue squarely. I should have returned one of Kate's telephone calls and said, "Kate, I'm very sorry, but there just isn't any point in our seeing one another. I'm going to marry Joe and I simply can't deal with your hostility toward him. It's obviously an impossible situation."

In such circumstances, the other person is bound to be aware that there are problems with the friendship, and if you're lucky he or she will just say, "I'm sorry, too," and let it go at that. But you also have to be prepared for tears, or for the person to say, "I don't understand," or even for a personal attack on you.

If the other person cries, I would say, "I'm sad about it, too, but it's better this way. There would just be more tears in the future, so I'm just going to say goodbye now." And that should be the end of the call. Prolonging it will just make things worse.

If the other person claims not to understand, I would say, "Well, that's the problem, isn't it? We don't understand each other anymore." You'll notice that it's *we* don't understand each other, not you don't understand me. Even if you feel very strongly that the other person is to blame, use the plural "we." Whatever you do, avoid explaining anything. Explanations in such circumstances will turn into recriminations before you can blink. Don't rehash the problems. If the other person starts to do so, say, "I'm sorry, but there's no point in discussing it. I'm very sorry." And end the conversation.

If you find yourself being attacked, say, "Excuse me, but this is exactly the problem. We aren't going to get anywhere discussing it. Let's just forget it."

Wouldn't it be easier, you may ask, to write a note. The answer is yes, but with a very large if attached. Write a note only if you can resist all temptation to elaborate, explain, or accuse. Keep it down to two or three sentences:

"We've obviously reached the point where our relationship isn't working anymore, and I think it's better to end it before things become more hurtful for both of us. I'll remember many pleasant times we had, and I wish you well."

That, or something like it, is all you have to say or should say. Anything beyond that, any rehashing whatsoever, you will later regret, and because words on paper can seem even harsher than words spoken aloud, you will also cause the other person even more pain. *Never* put your bad feelings about someone else in writing.

Getting married can bring an enforced end to some relationships, as was the case with my friendship with Kate. When a couple you are friends with get divorced, the chances of your losing one partner or the other as a friend are high. Sometimes, of course, there's no problem—you always did love him, hated her, or vice versa, and there's absolutely no question whose friendship you're going to retain. But often you will like both partners pretty much equally, and it can be a painful experience if one or the other demands that you be his or her friend alone, and cut off your relationship with the discarded spouse. Of course, nice people shouldn't make such demands or put you in that position, but nice people do it all the time when the divorce is a bitter one. My personal feeling is that the one who demands that you pledge your fealty to his or her cause is precisely the one to stay away from, in that they're trying to manipulate your feelings, not to mention showing that they don't really trust you. But there are exceptions that prove the rule, and the nice person has to recognize that people can get more than a little crazy during the throes of divorce.

So, if you are willing to accept one partner's demand that you cut off your relationship with the other, how can you do it nicely? Frankly, I doubt that you can do it nicely. The nice person has to admit that some of life's problems do not have pleasant solutions. I think the closest approximation to being nice about it is to say, "Well, I guess we're divorced, too, at least for the time being. Let's see what happens when things settle down." That holds out some small hope for the future. But sometimes you'll just have to grit your teeth and say, "Look, Bob, I'm afraid I have to take Linda's side in this." That's not going to make Bob feel good about it, or at all happy with you. But it may be the only way. Even so, I would strenuously avoid going into any detail as to why you have to take Linda's side. There's no need to turn the knife in the wound, Bob almost certainly knows exactly why.

Ending relationships is a lot easier for people who aren't nice than for those who are. The nice person would always prefer to alter the nature of the friendship, to make it work on a less intense and somewhat more casual plane. Certainly, that's what we should strive for. But if that doesn't work, it's better to end the friendship with a clean break than to let things go on in ways that will ultimately bring even greater pain or anger.

Part 2

LIFE'S BIG LITTLE PROBLEMS

8

Raving Jerks and Other Mutants

All of us, being human, have the capacity to turn into raving jerks at a moment's notice. One of my own most embarrassing descents into instant jerkhood took place at the White House. Joe had been asked to organize and preside over the musical entertainment at President and Mrs. Carter's first annual Christmas Party. During the day, the President himself took Joe and me on a tour of the family living quarters as well as several of the renowned upstairs rooms. It was in the Lincoln Bedroom that I opened my mouth and made one of those remarks one subsequently wishes had never passed one's lips. I said something about how impressive the room was. And then I added, trying to be amusing, "Think how great it will look once it's redecorated."

Since Washington was full of stories, some of them not very friendly, about the Carters' frugality, there was hardly anything less clever I could have said. The President didn't respond in words, but he did give me a glance as though he wondered whether he'd heard me right. In such situations, the only thing to do is just keep going, and I managed to burble something reasonably sociable. But it still gives me a sinking feeling to recall the moment.

While all of us are likely to make idiots of ourselves occasionally, we usually know when we've done it. True raving jerks, on the other hand, are seldom aware of the impact of their words or behavior. That's because they make a career of being raving jerks; so far as they're concerned, they're simply behaving normally and as usual. In the process, they provide a serious testing ground of the nice person's patience.

There are three major categories of raving jerks:

1. people who know it all;
2. people who think they're funny and aren't; and
3. people on egomaniacal crusades.

The one characteristic shared by all of these people is that they insist upon pressing themselves upon you when you aren't really interested in the least. Aside from that, the members of each group present special problems that require varying responses. Let's look at a number of techniques for dealing with the raving jerks of this world—nicely, when possible.

Mine Is Better

People who know it all always have the best doctor, lawyer, butcher, hairdresser, tailor, interior decorator, and caterer. The only thing they usually don't have is the best cleaning woman or housekeeper because the best servants can't stand them and leave with telltale regularity. People who know it all are constantly trying to tell you the secrets of life. Follow their advice, and everything will go like clockwork. Of course, they aren't really in the business of being helpful; they're just telling you how superior they are. Whatever you're doing is wrong; whatever they're doing is right.

As I've noted before, even the nicest people have some limits to the amount of patience they can muster, and there's no point in wasting too much of it on people who are continually putting you down. Your niceness is better applied where it's going to do some good. What you really want to do is to shut them up.

Turning off know-it-alls isn't easy, though. For one thing, they tend to have all the sensitivity of bulldozers, which makes it difficult to get through to them short of out-and-out rudeness. And you don't want to get actively rude, because that will just convince them more than ever of their own superiority; what's more, they will undoubtedly turn around and bad-mouth you from here to next Tuesday behind your back.

I find that one effective technique for dealing with know-it-alls is to suggest that they aren't telling you anything new. Such people's sense of superiority is based not only on their conviction that they do everything right, but also that they were the first on the block, in the office, or in their social set to get it right. If you can manage to indicate that you're already in possession of the information they are trying to press upon you, it usually takes a good deal of the wind out of their sails.

This doesn't mean that you actually have to have heard of the lawyer, doctor, restaurant, or house painting firm the know-it-all is recommending, of course. In fact, this is one of those cases in which a certain vagueness is especially effective. All you have to do is say, "Oh, yes, somebody mentioned him (the lawyer), her (the physician), it (the restaurant), or them (the house painters) a couple of weeks ago."

The know-it-all is likely at this point to want to know who you heard it from. I reply, "Funny, I can't remember

who it was. It was one of those half-overheard conversations."
This ploy frees you from the necessity of having to know
anything very specific. Some know-it-alls, however, still won't
give up. They'll ask, "Were they saying good things?"

Now you've got the know-it-all trapped. You can say,
"Well, I think whoever it was is using a different lawyer now,
but I don't remember anything negative. But obviously I
wasn't paying much attention."

A different lawyer? A different butcher? The know-it-all
will immediately begin to wonder if he or she is out of step
or behind the times. Somebody new? Does that mean somebody better? Am I making a fool of myself, the know-it-all
will ask himself or herself? And, in most cases, know-it-alls
will decide to keep their mouths shut at this point. You've
been perfectly polite, but you've planted a small seed of doubt
in their minds. Maybe there's something they don't know—a
suspicion that makes know-it-alls extremely uneasy. So long
as you can even suggest that possibility, you can get them
off your back.

Have You Heard the One . . .

Humor, happily, comes in many guises. There is the natural
humor, warm or silly or startled, that arises out of everyday
situations. There is the controlled created humor, whether
verbal or visual, of slapstick and farce. We have the witty
comment and the satirical send-up. Black humor has always
been with us and has been employed by some great artists to
profound effect. We also, of course, have sick humor and
dirty jokes.

Much humor has a cutting edge to it; it can pierce the
heart as well as warm it. That's why the nice person has to
be careful about humor. What may be perfectly appropriate

in one circumstance, and very funny, may be decidedly off-key in another. I remember all too well a remark I made in an airport waiting room preceding a flight to Los Angeles. I happen to hate flying, although I have to do a lot of it. Traveling on this particular flight were several top executives of both CBS and ABC, as well as a number of television reporters. As a group of us stood around chatting, I made the comment, "Lord, if this plane goes down, the success of Ted Turner's cable network is assured." Joe gave me a look, and later said, "You know, Pat, that wasn't funny. I know you were covering up your own nervousness, but other people could be nervous, too."

And he was exactly right. It wasn't at all a funny thing to say.

Yet a very similar comment made at "The Night of 100 Stars" at Radio City Music Hall brought the house down: Steve Allen suggested that if a bomb hit the place, the career of a certain much publicized but very untalented starlet would be assured. Since the likelihood of a bomb being dropped on Radio City that night was extremely remote, everyone was highly amused. One presumes that the starlet in question wasn't too happy when she heard about it, but it could also be said that she had been asking for it by the very nature of the self-promotion she'd embarked on.

Thus the nice person will try to stop and think before attempting to be funny. But, in self-defense, the nice person also needs to be prepared to deal with people who don't stop to think and whose "humor" is giving offense.

One problem is that a lot of people who think they're funny simply are not. Being funny is a gift that comes a great deal more easily to some people than to others. When someone who doesn't have the gift is working too hard at being funny, he or she can often seem insensitive or even plain rude. The best way to discourage someone whose humor you find offensive rather than amusing is simply not to laugh.

There *are* a few people who actually make their living by laughing; they're hired by television producers to sit in studio audiences and cackle regularly at anything remotely amusing. But none of the rest of us have the duty or responsibility to laugh at anything unless we're actually tickled by it. Nice people certainly do not have the duty to keep raving jerks happy by responding to offensive attempts at humor. The lack of an audible response will usually slow down such people very quickly. You can give a very quick twitch of the lips, with the mouth firmly closed, to indicate that you realize they are *trying* to be funny but that it just isn't working, but you should always avoid making any sound. Even the slightest chuckle will fuel their attempts. While there may be times when you have to go a step further and resort to the expressionless stare, I think it's usually a mistake to say, "I'm sorry, but I don't find that funny." The reason it's a mistake is that all too often the person will then proceed to *explain* why it's funny. Listening to someone try to explain why something is funny can be one of life's ghastlier small trials, and is to be avoided if at all possible.

The least funny people in the world, in my opinion, are those who bombard everyone they meet with sick, racist, or dirty jokes. If they find such stuff funny, that's their business, but they ought to find themselves friends who share their taste in humor and leave the rest of us alone. Richard Pryor, who I think is very funny, can get away with a lot because he is Richard Pryor. But there are five things that I think it's never nice for the armchair comedian to joke about: rape, abortion, the characteristics of any race or creed other than your own, physical deformities, and sex in general. Two of these five require further discussion.

Certain kinds of ethnic humor have a long-standing place in our society, going back to the days of vaudeville. But when you see comedians on television or in a nightclub, you'll notice that they make jokes only about their *own* ethnic background. Alan King has his Jewish mother jokes and Flip Wilson has his Geraldine impersonation, but they stay strictly out of one another's ethnic territory. The nice person would do well to follow their example. Remember that it's a small world: the very WASP Mr. Smith's wife may be Polish or Italian or Black or Jewish, and he may not at all appreciate hearing about how many of her countrymen or race or creed it takes to screw in a lightbulb.

The other subject that needs further discussion is sex. I myself use words I wouldn't say in front of my grandmother. That's not the point. And there's no doubt that human sexuality has its humorous side. That's not the point either. The point is that the nice person doesn't tell dirty jokes unless he or she is close enough to the person he or she is talking with to be damn sure that no offense is going to be taken, that in fact the person will be amused. And since a great many people, even in this tell-all age, are reticent about revealing their sexual pleasures or insecurities, you've got to be awfully close to someone indeed to be certain that you're not going to give offense.

But that's not going to stop the inveterate joke teller. There I am, standing with a small group of people at a large party. Someone has mentioned the Pope's visit to South America. And a raving jerk takes that as his cue to be funny. "Did you hear the one about the two nuns who were raped in their station-wagon," he begins. Oh boy, a religious dirty joke coming up, about rape no less.

That is my cue to leave. If there is any possibility of doing so, I say, "Excuse me," and walk away. Sometimes, of course, you're physically trapped. There's just no way you can get out of there. In that situation, I don't hesitate to say, "No, I haven't, and if you don't mind I'd rather not."

Yes, the joke teller is going to be embarrassed. But he's also going to be stopped dead in his tracks. And he deserves to be.

It Will Change Your Life

Your friend Lisa is a vegetarian—a very strict vegetarian. What's more she's a convert, who changed her dietary habits only a year ago. A few months back you had her to a buffet dinner party, at which you served a number of salads and vegetable dishes along with various meat offerings, and she was able to pick and choose what she ate. Tonight, however, you're having a sit-down dinner party, and partly as a gesture of friendship, partly for the challenge involved, you've produced an entirely vegetarian meal, beginning with a cold avocado soup and going on to an exotic vegetable curry served with a dozen different condiments.

Is Lisa grateful? Not exactly. Triumphant is more like it. When the other guests compliment you on the meal, Lisa takes the opportunity to launch into a half-hour dissertation on the philosophy, healthfulness, and sheer deliciousness of the vegetarian diet. She is on a crusade, attempting to convert everyone in sight. Her face is flushed, she's talking at the speed of light, and frankly, you could kill her.

Lisa has suddenly turned into a raving jerk.

Don't get me wrong. I have nothing against vegetarianism —I don't eat red meat myself. But I do have quite a lot against people who climb up on soapboxes and start screaming at me about their beliefs. Unfortunately, that kind of thing seems to be happening more and more often. Perfectly nice people suddenly get "into" something, and not only won't they stop talking about it, they won't even consider any other point of view. The range of causes people get caught up in is broad, from est to the Nuclear Freeze Movement. And while the philosophy or movement or form of therapy in question may be important to them, one can't help wondering how much good it's doing them when they turn into raving jerks over it.

That this should happen isn't so surprising, of course. A lot of people today don't like what they do and have no real relationship to the end product—they're just another drone in an enormous impersonal hive. Thus they fix on something, *anything,* that will provide them with a sense of identity and give them some emotional connections. It's the only avenue open to them for spouting off and feeling unique.

Feeling unique is important. Spouting off, however, means making a nuisance of yourself. Dealing with people who are on crusades, especially if you disagree with them or aren't much interested in their particular "religion," can be very difficult for the nice person. The nice person respects other people's right to their opinions and beliefs. But it's one thing when a proselytizer rings your front doorbell and tries to ply you with literature—whether you accept it or not, you can always close the door. It's quite another thing when someone you're seated next to on a transatlantic flight starts raving at you, or the virtual stranger seated next to you at a dinner party takes off into the verbal stratosphere. How in hell, you ask yourself, am I going to shut this one up?

It's not easy. It takes patience. But it can be done.

First. you have to resign yourself to the fact that there is no way to cut them off quickly. It will take a few minutes, at the least. Resignation is important, because if you allow your annoyance to show, it will just make matters worse.

The main rule is to say as little as possible yourself. Don't ask *any* questions. They expect questions, they know exactly what the questions will be, and they have page-long answers prepared for all of them.

If they ask *you* questions, make your answers as short and as vague as possible. "I really don't know." Or, "I'm not sure how I feel about that." You may know exactly, and have very strong feelings, but don't give in to the temptation to start spouting off yourself. If you do, you'll be in real trouble.

Above all, do not challenge them in any way. No matter how off-base their facts are or how wild some of their statements may be, dispute nothing.

What you have to realize is that raving jerks of the crusading sort are like wind-up toys. Anything you say, positive or negative, will be like giving a fresh turn to the key. If you just listen, look a little vague, and say practically nothing, they will eventually unwind. All those tightly coiled springs they've got inside them will loosen. And, finally, they will stop.

Remember that you too have the capacity to turn into a raving jerk. We all do.

9

Drunks, Nicotine Addicts, and Other "Smokers"

Millions of Americans continue to smoke cigarettes despite the warning that it may be dangerous to their health. Millions of Americans drink to excess. And millions of Americans smoke marijuana despite the fact that it's illegal, with cocaine use on the rise and constantly in the headlines. Sometimes perfectly nice people do all of these things, but other nice people object to them. And that presents serious problems when two nice people happen to be on opposite sides of the fence in regard to the consumption of any of these substances.

On the surface, it would seem that we're dealing with different levels of seriousness here: someone who blows cigarette smoke in your face, someone who's too drunk to drive home safely, and someone who's breaking a rarely enforced law, are creating problems of different magnitudes. But it's not as simple as that. Some people who are allergic to cigarette smoke or simply find it a "filthy habit," get a lot more exercised about the stranger who's smoking at the next table in a crowded restaurant than they do about the friend who gets so drunk he has to be put to bed in the guestroom. Many people who smoke pot on a daily basis speak disparagingly of people who drink too much as "lushes," and simply brush aside the fact that their own habit is against the law. The fact is that we're dealing with an area in which actual health concerns, holier-than-thou attitudes, rationalizations, and a good deal of out-and-out irrationality inevitably knock up against one another, with results that are often difficult to cope with.

Let's see if we can sort out some of the conflicts involved by examining:

1. The protocol of smoking
2. Coping with drunken guests
3. Turning off the turn-ons

Nicotine Fits

Although I don't smoke myself, I have no objection to other people doing so. If you're going to work in a television news division, you'd better not object, because the amount of cigarette smoking that goes on in that high-pressure environment would keep an entire county of tobacco farmers in business.

But an increasing number of people do object to smoking. While smokers themselves tend to be suspicious of such claims, a lot of people really are allergic to cigarette smoke— it makes their eyes water, their throats close up, and causes genuine physical discomfort. Anyone with that kind of allergic reaction has the perfect right, anytime and anyplace, to ask people please not to smoke. They should, however, make it clear that they have an allergy. Smokers, after all, are addicted to tobacco, and they're going to find it easier to deal with the fact that they can't indulge themselves, and be nicer about it, if they're given a good medical reason for abstaining for a while.

There are other people who object to smoking because they believe that even the inhaling of smoke from somebody else's cigarette is going to affect their health. The problem here is that while some medical studies seem to confirm that even secondary inhalation can be detrimental, there are other studies that contradict such findings. Smokers, of course, tend to believe the latter studies, which absolve them of responsibility for poisoning their fellow men, and can get testy on the subject. I think it's a grave mistake for a person to ask someone else not to smoke and then add, "Don't you know you're poisoning me, too?" That's picking a fight. You're much better off telling a white lie and claiming to be allergic, even if you aren't.

There are also, unfortunately, nonsmokers who are simply smug about their clean living, and who have appointed themselves reformers of the addicted. They will turn to perfect strangers at bus stops and in bank lines and say, "You really shouldn't smoke, you know." In such situations, the smoker has every right to be annoyed, and shouldn't be censored for coming back with a line like, "You really shouldn't talk to strangers, you know." Not especially nice, but deserved. There are a lot of people in the world of television who would like to say something of that sort to Tony Randall. While one can respect his views, he has been known to carry his antismoking crusade to the point of treating smokers as though they were diseased animals. You don't get people to "kick the habit" by insulting them—you just drive them to smoking in closets and washrooms.

On the whole, though, the burden of being nice is on the smoker's shoulders. In restaurants, other people's offices, and other people's homes, the nice smoker will ask if it's all right to do so. Of course, if the person whose territory you're on lights up, or if there are several ashtrays prominently displayed, it's not necessary to ask. There's another side to this coin, however. Unless a person is truly allergic, I don't think he or she has the right to ask other people not to smoke in their own offices or homes. That's just plain pushy.

The nice person who smokes has to recognize that there are some people who are allergic to smoke and others who find the habit distasteful, and that it's always a good idea to ask. In return, however, the nonsmoker has to realize that because cigarettes are addictive, not smoking can be both psychologically and physically distressing to the smoker. This is an area where some compromise is necessary on both sides, on the part of those who throw fits about nicotine as well as those who have nicotine fits.

You Can't Lock Them in the Hall Closet

Years ago I came very close to marrying a man who had a serious drinking problem. The alcoholism of someone you love is a problem that far transcends the question of how to be a nice person, and is better left to experts in the field. Most of us, however, run into the lesser but still vexing difficulty of coping with the drunken dinner guest from time to time, and it does seem appropriate to discuss that kind of circumstance within the context of this book.

Putting aside medical arguments (and disagreements) about what level of alcohol consumption is indicative of alcoholism, it seems evident from social experience that some people can drink a great deal and still retain an astonishing amount of control over their behavior, while other people who drink a lot less go to pieces, turn nasty, get sick, and generally cause problems. The question I'd like to look at is this: What do you do, as a host or hostess, when a guest gets thoroughly drunk in your home? How do you handle the problem nicely?

You can't, unfortunately, simply lock them in the hall closet until it's time to go home. I have been at a party at which a guest passed out in the bathroom, with the door locked from the inside; nobody missed him for a while, and it would have been convenient to simply leave him there, but as the apartment had only one bathroom, it was eventually necessary to jimmy the lock. Indeed, drunks are usually very insistent about making their presence felt, either as the life or bane of the party. There are several steps the nice person can take, however, in order to:

1. keep people from getting drunk,
2. handle people who get drunk, and
3. get the drunk home in one piece.

A lot of people bring the problem of the drunken guest down on themselves by inviting guests for seven o'clock and then not getting around to serving dinner until nine or nine-thirty. This is asking for trouble. If the host or hostess has that much difficulty getting dinner on the table, or can't bear to leave his or her guests long enough to get things organized in the kitchen, they should try giving a different kind of party, say a buffet for which all the food is prepared ahead of time. I don't think the cocktail hour should ever last longer than the time that is built into the phrase: one hour.

Applying that rule in actual practice isn't always easy, though. For one thing, you'll run afoul of guests who make it a habit to be "fashionably late." I think you have to put your foot down on this one. Anybody who is more than forty minutes late to a dinner party isn't being fashionable but rude. I firmly believe that the nice person has the right to go ahead and serve dinner to the other guests at the planned time, even if that means that people who want to make a grand entrance have to scuttle into the dining room and take their places in the middle of the first course. Now, of course, if you were planning to serve dinner at eight, and guests call to tell you that their car has broken down and they won't be able to get there until eight-fifteen, it's incumbent upon the nice person to delay dinner a little. But if the person who's calling is going to be really late, it's incumbent on him or her to suggest you go ahead and eat. It is both sensible and perfectly nice to take people up on that kind of suggestion. Otherwise, it's going to mean serving another couple of rounds of drinks, and the potential for somebody getting thoroughly sloshed is going to rise dramatically.

When I know that someone is likely to be late, I always invite them to arrive a half-hour earlier than anyone else. (I also make it a point to be ready for them to arrive at that earlier hour, just in case they're in the process of reforming themselves, or because they're suspicious that they've been invited at an earlier hour on purpose and want to make clear that they know what you're pulling on them. In the latter case, you can always say that you invited them early because you thought it would be nice to talk for a while before the mob arrived. Obviously, though, you have to be careful: you can't invite people who know one another well, or who might come in the same car, to arrive at different times.)

On the other side of the situation, I invite people who I know are likely to get drunk for a half-hour later than anyone else. That gives them less time to pour gin down their throats before you can get some stabilizing food into their systems. This ploy doesn't always work, for the simple reason that the drunk in question may well have a couple of extra martinis at home before setting out for the evening's festivities. Nevertheless, it's not *your* liquor they've gotten plotzed on, they were already pretty far gone when they arrived. And that's important for your own peace of mind later in the evening in taking steps to handle the situation. If you're not responsible, it's easier to take a firm hand without feeling guilty about it.

The first thing to remember about the drunk is that he

or she is out of control and has turned into a raving jerk. There is no more point in disagreeing with or challenging a drunk than there is debating a perfectly sober raving jerk who's bending your ear about some crusade he's on. Thus the same rules apply as were outlined in chapter 8. The jolly drunk is obviously easier to tolerate than the surly drunk. With surly drunks, the main responsibility of the host or hostess is to prevent the drunk from insulting the other guests. I wouldn't hesitate to interrupt the drunk in mid-sentence, or remove the target from his or her vicinity by escorting the person who's being attacked to another room under any pretext that can be devised.

Most important of all, though, is to try to get someone else at the party to take on the job of dealing with the drunk. Often, the spouse or another friend of the drunk will take on this responsibility automatically. If that doesn't happen, ask someone to do it. On the surface that may not seem like a nice thing to do—asking someone to take on a difficult and perhaps unpleasant job. But the fact is that you're in the worst position of anybody to try to handle the drunk. It's *your* hospitality that the drunk is abusing. In the back of his or her mind, the drunk knows that, and, trying to deny the guilt he or she feels at spoiling your party, is less likely to take admonishments from you than from anybody else present. So leave it to somebody else to tell the drunk he's made a fool of himself. Fortunately, there are a lot of people who like to play the hero in situations like this—unpleasant though the job may be, it gives them a feeling of being nice, competent, and trusted to take it on. It makes people feel good about themselves to play the good samaritan sometimes, and this is a situation in which you should take advantage of that psychological truth.

When it comes to getting the drunk home in one piece, you should also call on other people. Unless there is a spouse or close friend of the drunk's also attending, someone who is used to taking charge of getting the drunk home, I would call on the person or persons who know the drunk *least* well to take on this chore. I know that sounds peculiar—never mind unfair to the person whose lap you're dumping the problem in. But the truth is that the drunk is often willing to go along quite docilely with someone he or she doesn't know well, but will put up a fight with someone to whom there is a closer emotional connection. Where there is a close connection, the drunk may feel that he or she is being judged, patronized, or "scolded," and can become even more difficult to handle. What's more, the relative stranger is likely to stay calmer simply because of the fact that there is no emotional coloration to the relationship. The psychological factors involved here are complex, but they parallel the reasons why AA—a congregation of strangers—can often help alcoholics where family and friends have failed.

Finally, of course, it goes without saying that if someone regularly gets drunk when he or she comes to a party, the time has come to think about extricating yourself from the friendship, of exercising the nice person's right to say, "I don't need this anymore," as discussed in chapter 7.

What's Wrong With a Little Grass?

At a party Joe and I attended not long ago, a well-known young actor politely refused the offer of an after-dinner brandy and then proceeded to open his silver cigarette case, take out a joint of marijuana, light it up, and offer it around. There were a dozen guests, and three of them, somewhat hesitantly, partook of the ritual, passing the joint around among them. But other guests, and the hostess herself, were clearly uncomfortable. Within fifteen minutes, the party had divided sharply into two segments, the marijuana smokers enjoying their grass off in one corner while the rest of us sipped our brandy and coffee at the other end of the large living room.

Fine, some of you may say, everybody's having a good time "doing their thing."

I'm afraid not.

Let's get something straight here. If anybody wants to smoke grass in the privacy of their own homes, hotel rooms, or behind the barn, that's up to them. I haven't an objection in the world. It's also okay by me if people smoke in other people's homes, provided that the hosts and everybody else present are comfortable with the situation.

But the nice person doesn't break out a joint at somebody else's home without asking, unless it's known to be fully acceptable.

Let's skip all the arguments about whether marijuana should or should not be legalized. There are both sensible and utterly irrational arguments on both sides of that question. I've heard brilliant defenses of both positions. I've also heard a great deal of hysterical drivel from proponents and opponents. The point is that the matter remains undecided, and so long as it does, the smoking of marijuana remains *illegal*.

In some states you can go to jail.

I know, people smoke it in movie houses and parks and even walking down the street. I know, the cops more often than not look the other way in some localities, especially large cities where they've got far more drastic things to worry about.

Still, you can get arrested. And that makes a lot of people very nervous, including a surprising number of people who smoke pot anyway.

Forget about the debates. If you smoke pot (or for that matter take cocaine), do you, as a nice person, really want to make other people who don't partake uncomfortable or even actively upset? If your answer is, "Well, if people could only see how harmless it is, certainly no worse than drinking and maybe better, we'd get it legalized in no time and then there'd be no problem," then you're on a crusade and we know what that means.

No, I'm sorry, but nice people who smoke pot don't just take out a joint and light up with total unconcern at other people's homes any more than nice people who are nudists take off their clothes and parade around naked at suburban barbecues.

No.

Okay, with that settled, I'd like to address the other side of the question. What if you disapprove of pot, you're worried about your children turning on to drugs, it simply makes you uncomfortable, or you're plain old-fashioned and think the world is rapidly going to hell in a handbasket? What do you do when somebody takes out a joint in your presence without asking?

What you do is ask the person to refrain.

Yes, that can be difficult. If you do, you've immediately painted yourself as a square, a reactionary, or an old fogy. But if the thought pops into your head, "I don't like this, but if I don't let it happen, they'll say I'm a square," just remember that you're being coerced—culturally blackmailed.

Personally, I don't give a damn whether I'm "with it" or not. I'm not comfortable with people smoking marijuana in my house and that's all there is to it. I try to be nice about it. I say, "I'm sorry, but we're really not comfortable with that." I may add, "Because of the kids." But I'm also willing to go on and say, "Please put that out."

If I go to a party at someone else's house, and marijuana is being smoked, fine, it's none of my business. But on my own territory it's different. The nice person has every right to make the rules in his or her own home.

10

"The Man Who Came to Dinner" and Other Houseguests

There are few better ways to find out what friends are *really* like than to have them as houseguests. Or, as it sometimes turns out, worse ways. When you have someone as a houseguest for the first time, you invariably discover a lot of things about the person you didn't know before. It's a twenty-four-hour experience. You discover what people are like in the morning. They may be slugabeds, or rise at the crack of dawn and crash around the house like a demolition crew. They may be breakfast grumps or blue-streakers, talking your ear off while you're still semicomatose. Surprises are inevitable. Your friend Alice, whose own apartment usually looks as though it could use a good going over by the Sanitation Department, turns out to be extremely neat on someone else's territory, like the child who's a terror at home but behaves like an angel when staying overnight at a fourth-grade friend's house. Your impeccably tailored friend Bob, on the other hand, abandons his shoes overnight in the living room, drapes wet towels over the maple footboard of his bed, and leaves the bathroom looking as though it had been hit by a well-aimed grenade. There are people who fall asleep after dinner, practically in midsentence, and people who want to discuss world events until 3:00 A.M. There are people who have nightmares and let out terrifying screams in the middle of the night, waking you from a deep sleep to face the possibility that a murder is taking place down the hall.

Some houseguests are likely to make *you* want to murder them in their beds. They seem to be under the impression that you are a hotel proprietor, and demand round-the-clock service. Or they're so happy to be staying with you that you can't get away from them for ten seconds; they won't go out by themselves to buy a pack of cigarettes, and insist upon tagging along to the butcher, the baker, or the candlestick-maker when *you* go out. They have their own car but they want to come along in yours, telling you when to go to the beach and when it's time to go home. And then there are the couples who wake the entire household, including your children, at two in the morning by indulging in an angry domestic spat or, even worse, extremely vocal sex.

Fortunately, there are also ideal houseguests. Two of my favorite guests are Morley Safer of "60 Minutes" and his wife Jane. They can be by turns enormously entertaining and utterly unobtrusive, lend a helping hand or stay out from under foot, take care of themselves or join in a group endeavor with great enthusiasm—and they do all these things at just the right times. Morley also makes great Apple Betty, unasked. They're more than welcome in our house at any time, not least because they are sterling examples of how the nice person ought to behave as a houseguest.

But since a lot of otherwise nice people—and many who, one discovers to one's sorrow, aren't as nice as they should be—can turn out to be utterly impossible houseguests, I'd like to look at how one can handle, nicely, some of the more intractable problems that houseguests may present:

1. The unmarried couple who want to stay in the same room.
2. Clinging vines.
3. The man-who-came-to-dinner syndrome.

Affairs of the Heart

Unmarried people who either live together or look upon themselves as a couple are increasingly common these days. And many people think nothing of inviting an unmarried couple—even a gay couple—for the weekend and putting them up in the same room or bed. But other hosts are not happy with that situation, because of concerns about their children's reaction, because they have more conservative values, or because the visiting couple includes their own son or daughter home from college with a "date."

Here, once again, the context can be all-important. If you *don't* feel comfortable about putting up an unmarried couple in the same rom, how can you deal with the situation nicely? Suppose you have a summer home and you'd like to invite your good friends Jill and Roger for a weekend. They've been living together for two years, but because you have two kids of adolescent age, you don't want to have Jill and Roger sleeping in the same room. If you have two spare rooms, there's no logistical problem. But there may well be a personal problem, in that Jill and Roger are going to want to *share* a room, even though they realize it's perfectly possible to tiptoe down the hall after lights out.

In a situation of this kind, I think it's vital to make matters clear from the start, explaining that you're going to put the couple in separate rooms when you issue your invitation. If you spring that arrangement on them when they arrive, they're going to be annoyed. They're going to look at one another and think, "Unh-oh, we shouldn't have come." Because they may indeed not want to accept if they're going to be separated, they should be given a chance to decline the invitation gracefully. That means that instead of inviting them by telephone, you should write a note, which will give them time to talk the matter over, as well as avoiding your getting involved in any first-hand debates as to whether the fact that they live together means they're "as good as married."

There shouldn't be any need to club them over the head with the arrangement you have in mind, however. You can say in your note that you've got two lovely rooms for them, with Jill's facing the lighthouse and Roger's overlooking the bay. Nice people can take a hint—usually. But if Jill calls you to give you an argument about it, saying with a little laugh that she didn't realize you were so old-fashioned, don't let yourself be intimidated. Tell her it's because of the kids and suggest that perhaps they'd rather book rooms for themselves at a local motel or inn, or come just for a day. If an unmarried couple turns down the offer of separate rooms in your home, and prefers to stay at a motel instead, I don't think you have any obligation to foot the bill. On the other hand, if you have only one spare room in the first place, and suggest from the start that they stay at a motel, the nice thing to do is to say, "We'll put you up at a motel," meaning that you will pay for it.

A different problem is presented by the college-age (or even older) son or daughter who wants to bring a "friend" of the opposite sex home for a visit. Some very liberated parents may not mind having sonny and his girl friend sleeping together in the son's bed, but the great majority of parents, even today, seem to find that idea upsetting. With a daughter, feelings are likely to be even stronger. Once again,

I think it's important to deal with the problem right at the start, the moment you're informed by Sam Jr. that he's bringing his friend Suzy home with him. Don't "just hope" Sam will have the sense to know that he and Suzy aren't going to bunk in together. You have to—and have a perfect right to—put it on the line. But the potential tensions involved can be alleviated by getting the son or daughter to participate in the decision as to who is going to sleep where: "Do you want to give Suzy your room and share your younger brother's bed? Or would you rather sleep on the sofa?" If it's at all possible to set up this kind of choice, giving the college kid the chance to help solve the problem, the possibilities for disgruntlement are lessened. If you live in an apartment with limited space, one solution may be to have your own child sleep over at a friend's house, while his or her friend stays with you. But make your kid a party to the solution, so that he feels he's being treated as a grown-up rather than an irresponsible child.

Just remember that as a nice person you are *never* obliged to arrange things so that other people can have sex under your roof if you're not comfortable with the situation. If it doesn't bother you, fine. But if it does, never lose sight of the fact that it's *your* house.

Oh, I'll Go With You

Some houseguests seem to lose their sense of themselves as independent human beings when visiting friends or relatives. They become clinging vines, entwining themselves around you like some form of mutant ivy in a grade C horror movie. This can become oppressive, to say the least.

They won't do anything on their own or allow you to do anything without them. Some people do this out of misplaced niceness—they're afraid that if they do anything on their own you'll think they were looking for free bed and board instead of coming to see *you*. With many others, it's simply a matter of insecurity. They're afraid they'll get lost on the subways, mugged, or raped if they're visiting you in a big city, or if it's the country, they'll say they don't know the roads or worry that the locals won't be friendly. And you find yourself nominated as round-the-clock bodyguard and tour guide. Even at home they won't let you alone for a minute. If you go into the kitchen, they're right there behind you. Say you're going to pick some tomatoes from the garden for lunch and they volunteer to "help." You don't want help, you want five minutes of privacy, of not having to entertain them, of not having to be nice, damn it.

When saddled with houseguests of this sort, you simply have to face up to the fact that you're not going to get them to do anything on their own, no matter how many taxis you offer to call for them, or road maps you draw for them. You have to concentrate instead on escaping them. I take naps. I may not even close my eyes, I may read or do some paperwork instead, but I announce that I'm taking a nap and I go into the bedroom and close the door. Some people, I'm sure, have thought it was rude of me to disappear for an hour, but the only alternative was to start screaming, "Leave me alone." Naps are the nicer way.

I also develop devious schemes to get out of the house without them. This isn't easy. Short of accompanying you to the dentist (an unlikely appointment on a Sunday afternoon, anyway), the clinging vine generally seems to view any and all outings in your company as "fun." It won't work to tell the clinging vine that you have a lot of small errands to run and that he or she would be bored. Clinging vines are convinced they'd be a lot more bored waiting for you to return home. You've got to come up with something that the clinging vine really won't want to do or will understand to be a "private" situation. The necessity of stopping by to see a friend (whom the clinging vine has never met) who has just returned from the hospital following a serious operation is one possibility. Yes, of course that's a white lie—perhaps even tinged with gray. Never mind, in desperate circumstances, even nice people have the right to take fairly desperate measures.

When dealing with clinging vines, I think it's permissible for the nice person to use almost any ploy that will work to get away by yourself now and again. Because if you don't, your irritation is going to reach the point where you can't control it anymore, and then you're likely to do or say something that really isn't nice. The nice person always has the right to preserve his or her sanity.

Just Until I Get Settled

Kaufman and Hart's *The Man Who Came to Dinner* is deservedly one of the classic comedies of the American theater. But if it happens to you that someone comes for dinner, or a weekend, and ends up staying for ten days or two weeks because of accidental circumstances, it can end up being anything but a laughing matter. One summer, some very wealthy friends from Bermuda were spending six weeks sailing their yacht up and down the New England coast, and we invited them to stop off and spend a weekend with us on Cape Cod. Unhappily, there was a severe storm the day before they arrived, and the mainmast of the yacht was broken off in the course of it. Our friends asked if they could lay over until the mast was replaced. Of course we said yes. Little did we realize that it would be ten days before a new mast was in place and they could continue their ocean wanderings. Considering their wealth, I think it might have been nice of them to suggest that they move into a motel or rent a beach cottage, but they did not, and as a result I took a lot of naps and invented a wide variety of excuses to get out of the house.

Fortunately, that kind of man-who-came-to-dinner situation is relatively uncommon, although it can certainly occur quite easily in parts of the country affected by hurricanes, blizzards, cyclones, and other natural disasters. Since there's not much one can do in such situations but grin and bear it, I'd like to discuss instead another kind of man-who-came-to-dinner syndrome that seems to be on the increase. It is a problem that younger single people appear to encounter with surprising frequency.

An old friend who's been living in another part of the country telephones and announces that he or she has decided to move to the city you live in—New York, Los Angeles, Houston—in order to take advantage of greater career opportunities or just as a change of pace. Can your friend stay with you while finding a job or an apartment?

The problem here is that if you say yes, you are extending an extremely open-ended invitation. Neither jobs nor apartments are always easy to come by, and it could be several weeks or even a couple of months before your houseguest manages to get settled on his or her own. What you're going to get isn't a houseguest but a roommate.

Many nice people, against their better judgment, appear to find it difficult to say no to this kind of proposition. It's a good friend, he or she needs help, maybe has lost a job due to the state of the economy—how *can* you say no? Well, you may not want to say no, but I'd be very careful to qualify your yes in several ways.

I'd start by indicating that the invitation isn't completely open-ended: "Well, I can certainly put you up for a week or two, and if you aren't settled by then, maybe we can find a place for you to sublet for a while or dig up somebody who needs a roommate." Then I would ask the friend, right up front, what his or her financial situation is. Yes, I know, I've said it isn't nice to ask people how much money they make or have, but this is a different situation—the person is moving in with you, even if only temporarily, and you have every right to know if they can help pay for food, their share of the telephone bill, etc. By asking, you are also indicating, without being too blatant about it, that you'll expect them to chip in on expenses.

If you fail to indicate that the invitation isn't open-ended, and avoid the question of finances, you will be leaving yourself wide open for trouble. This is one case in which the nice thing to do, for everybody's sake, is to get the cards on the table. Otherwise you may find yourself supporting your friend for weeks on end, caught up in a situation that can only be resolved by the unpleasant task of throwing the person out.

If it's agreed that the friend is only going to stay with you for a week or two, you may want to play host during that period, and treat the friend largely as a guest. But I think it's a lot smarter, under the circumstances, to involve your friend in the daily tasks of shopping, cooking, washing dishes, and doing laundry. It's perfectly nice to say, "Let's go to the supermarket," or "Shall we do laundry tonight?"

After a number of days have passed, and your friend hasn't shown any initiative about finding someplace else to stay in the near future, I would take an active hand in doing something about it yourself, calling other friends to see if they know of a place, suggesting agencies, and so on. If this is done tactfully, it will be taken as a way of helping out, rather than being seen as trying to get rid of the person. I wouldn't go so far as to start circling newspaper ads, for example—that's a little blatant. Besides, it's a tactic you should keep in reserve in case your friend proves unmovable, and starts asking for "another few days."

But it shouldn't come to that—not if you've taken the precaution of putting some limits to the length of the proposed stay in the first place.

As in other problematical situations involving houseguests, it's what you failed to get straight prior to the visit that will get you in trouble. It's your house, and you have the right to make the rules. But you have to let the other person know what those rules are. The nice person should never be afraid to make clear what he or she expects from visitors. And the nice visitor should never take offense at being told what those expectations are.

11

Adults Only, or the Party's Rated "R"

The nice person has the right to say, "No Children Allowed." In fact, the nice person has a right to dislike children.

Dislike children? Why that's unnatural!

Oh no it isn't.

Children can be adorable, fascinating, funny, moving, and in general the light of our lives. But children can also be little monsters. Even the nicest child is going to talk back, ask incessant questions, be embarrassingly candid, destroy precious objects, and at times behave in an altogether uncivilized manner. What's more there are many children who are almost never nice. You may have noticed that there are a lot of utterly impossible adults walking around, and you can bet they were always that way. Awful people start training to be awful before they can walk. It may not be their fault. They may have awful, incompetent, or brutal parents. But awful is awful.

A few years back the son and daughter of friends who

live a few blocks away came to visit for an afternoon. They destroyed a pool table, sent one of my stepsons into hysterics, tried to beat up another, and created total havoc. They're never setting foot in our house again, and if we can no longer call their parents friends as a result, so be it.

Much as I love my own kids, I am never surprised to discover that there are nice people who can't stand children. Sometimes their reasons go back to their own childhoods. Several times I have heard people say, "I didn't like children when *I* was a child and I'm not about to change my mind." I fully respect people who say that they aren't going to have children because they aren't interested and wouldn't be good parents, anyway. If more people were willing to admit to themselves that they wouldn't be good parents, then there would be far fewer rotten children—and eventually rotten adults—in the world.

Even people who like children very much don't want them around all the time. There are occasions that are clearly "adults only," and children will be out of place, in the way, and a general nuisance. Yet people are often tempted to take their children along regardless. Even when they know that the person who has invited them has no use for children, the attiude is often one of: "Well, they'll like *my* kids." The trouble is that people who dislike and avoid children quite naturally have no idea how to deal with them. So no matter how proud we may be of our kids, it is wise to remember that there are people who would rather avoid contact with anyone under eighteen. Nice people should not be in the business of trying to change other people's prejudices by force—and bringing along your children unannounced will certainly be seen by those who dislike children as a kind of preemptive strike.

What's more, people who do like children, and have children of their own, may be equally annoyed at having someone else's kids forced upon them in certain circumstances.

This is an area in which we need guidelines on both sides of the coin, for those who like to take their children everywhere, and for those who want to discourage that tendency:

1. Never take your children along without forewarning.
2. If children are brought along unexpectedly to your house or party, remember that it's your territory.
3. Ways to discourage people from bringing their children.

You Can't Park Them in the Driveway

"It's not as though we're going to the Greens' for a family picnic, Joe. It's a dinner party for Frank Sinatra."

The party was being given by the late Bill Green and his wife Judy at their sprawling Westchester estate, replete with helicopter pad, Olympic-size swimming pool, and private trout pond. Frank Sinatra was not only the guest of honor but also the chef for the evening—preparing spaghetti for eighty people. Joe thought it would be great fun for Joe Jr. and Nicholas to see the estate and meet the legendary singer.

I thought it was a terrible idea.

Joe's rationale was twofold. First, he had only recently gained custody of the boys, and he could hardly bear to let them out of his sight. Second, I was pregnant with Joe's and my first child, and Joe thought the boys possibly felt threatened by this on-coming event and he wanted to do something special for them.

I still thought it was a terrible idea. I told him that you don't take childlren, uninvited and unnanounced, to anybody's party, and certainly not to this one.

Wisely, Joe had not told the boys yet that we might take them along, so if I managed to dissuade him from pursuing the idea, I wouldn't be cast in the role of cruel stepmother.

There are some husbands—or wives—who would indeed have told the kids in advance, before discussing it with the stepparent, thus creating an unpleasant situation by putting the stepparent in the position of either having to agree or play the villain. Not a nice thing to do, of course, in any situation.

Joe is much too secure to stoop to that kind of manipulation, so I was free to press my case. I pointed out that he was almost as inseparable from his new Porsche as he was from the boys, but that the car, unlike the kids, could be parked in the driveway.

Joe, as is sometimes the case, was not to be moved. I was in a rage, but I gave in for a very practical reason. Joe knew the directions to get to the Greens' and I didn't.

Another question then arose. Should we telephone in advance to let the Greens know what was in store for them? That certainly would be the nice thing to do—even the "correct" thing to do in the old-fashioned sense. If I were to make the call, I would make sure that the matter was presented in a way that would allow Judy Green to politely suggest that it didn't seem like a very good idea. But Joe, knowing I would handle it that way, would insist on making the call himself. Charmer that he is, *he* would manage to put things so that our hosts would find it very difficult to say anything other than, "Why, yes, of course." Besides, I didn't want to make the call myself—it hadn't been my idea in the first place to take the boys along.

Joe didn't feel it was necessary to call, and so we simply arrived with the boys in tow. On the basis of my right to refuse unfair responsibility. I let Joe do the explaining. As it happens, Joe is very skilled at being disarming. Judy Green is also a very nice person, and only a fleeting expression of shock crossed her face.

The boys were the only children there, of course. I was still steaming, but after a while I noticed that the boys had disappeared. Good, I thought, they've gone off to amuse themselves somewhere out of the way.

Not a bit of it. They were in the kitchen, distracting Mr. Sinatra from the task of preparing his spaghetti. He was having a wonderful time and didn't seem to mind in the least, but it was getting on towards ten o'clock, the hors d'oeuvres had long since disappeared, and there were eighty very hungry people waiting to be fed.

In consultation with Judy Green, I managed to get the boys out of the kitchen and dispatched to a basement playroom. They had a fine time down there, but, as we learned later, they ran into a small problem. There was no bathroom adjacent to the playroom, and when they climbed the stairs to find one, they discovered that they were locked in. I'm sure that wasn't intentional, but it seemed a fitting climax to the saga. Fortunately, a passing servant heard them banging on the door, and released them from their luxurious little dungeon.

There's no doubt that the boys had fun. But it is also true that their fooling around in the kitchen delayed dinner for eighty people by at least half an hour, perhaps more. They didn't belong there in the first place, and the evening's events only convinced me more than ever that one should never take children along uninvited.

If Judy Green had wanted them there, she would have invited them. If it had been an afternoon party, with the possibility of playing outdoors on the estate grounds, it would have been a very different party and she might have asked a lot of children. But under the circumstances, she was exercising her right to say, "No Children Allowed."

When children aren't invited, they aren't wanted. You can be sure of it.

If you have an infant whom you don't want to leave with a baby-sitter, it's not out of line to ask if you can bring the child along to a small party given by close friends. An infant can be tucked away to sleep in a bedroom. But if it's a large party, I think it's better not to go. And as soon as the child begins to walk, remember that he or she is more than likely to get into some kind of mischief. Your child is your responsibility, and if that means that you have to stay home yourself, that's an aspect of your responsibility that has to be faced.

Uninvited, unwanted.

A *Playboy* Lesson

On the other side of the coin, what do you do if someone does bring an uninvited child to a party you're giving?

The answer is: Do what you damn please. It's your territory and you're dealing with an unwelcome intruder.

It's perfectly possible to be nice about it, in one sense, and at the same time teach someone a lesson.

A friend I'll call Sarah recalls an occasion a number of years ago that still has her chuckling. She was giving a cocktail party for a number of friends. Among those she invited was her Aunt Lillian, whose nine-year-old grandson Paul happened to be visiting her. Sarah was perfectly well aware of Paul's presence in town—she'd had him over for ice cream and cookies the previous week. But this was a cocktail party, and she made no mention of Paul when she invited his grandmother. Nine-year-olds were mature enough to look after themselves for a couple of hours, in her opinion.

But when Lillian arrived, there was Paul, too. Sarah said, "Oh, hello, Paul. I didn't realize you were coming. I'm afraid this is just going to be a bunch of boring adults." The nice person has to remember that it's not the uninvited child's fault that he's there. He probably didn't even want to come.

Sarah's next step was to offer Paul a small glass of wine.

His grandmother, who didn't drink at all, was horrified. Sarah said that an ounce of wine wasn't going to hurt him in the least, French children drank it all the time.

After he'd had his token cocktail, Sarah escorted Paul upstairs to the bedroom of her youngest son, who was away at college. She told him that he could look at any books or magazines he wanted, but to put them back where they came from. Exploring the room, Paul discovered years of back issues of *Playboy* magazine in the closet, which he proceeded to spend a very enlightening hour and a half thumbing through.

The next morning, Sarah received a telephone call from Paul's grandmother, who had discovered how the boy had kept himself entertained. She was, she said, shocked.

Sarah, administering the coup de grace, said, "Well, it was an adult party, Lillian. What's more, I'm sure Paul had a wonderful time."

Sarah notes that Paul, now in his twenties, remembers the day with fond pleasure.

Sarah had done, as she saw it, the right thing her way.

When an uninvited child is forced upon you, remember that it's your territory. The child should be made to feel at ease—it's not his fault that he's there. But there is no reason not to administer a small lesson to the person who brought him.

Saying No in the Nicest Way

What do you do when people ask you, or tell you, that they are bringing along a child, or worse, children, whom you haven't invited?

You start by trying to make the person see that it's not a good idea. The most effective way to do that, and the nicest, is to look at it from the point of view of the child who's being foisted upon you.

For example, suppose you have invited a good friend to a dinner party. You're not giving the party at home but at a nearby restaurant. Your friend says that she'll be bringing along her son Dennis. Dennis is a very bright, very talkative, and very rambunctious thirteen-year-old. You have children of your own, but they're much younger and wouldn't be included in the party under any circumstances. Dennis, however, is on that borderline between childhood and adulthood that leads his mother to conclude that he's ready to break bread with grownups on any and all occasions.

I've been faced with this problem a number of times, and I eventually found a solution that works nine times out of ten.

I say, "Well, Dennis is more than welcome to stay here at the house and eat with my kids."

I have thus issued an invitation, even if not the desired one. But having done so, it makes it more difficult for Dennis's mother to try for an upgraded invitation to the adult dinner.

Then, quickly, before she has a chance to think about how to angle for a better deal, I add, "But I think Dennis would find that awfully boring."

Obviously, I have Dennis's best interests at heart, but it should be perfectly clear that there's no way he is going to spend the evening with the rest of us.

Of course, there are some people who simply can't take a hint. If Dennis's mother were to go on to say, "Well, I'm sure he'd have a wonderful time with us," I would forget about trying to soften the blow and move on to a more direct objection, such as, "I really don't think it's appropriate for Dennis to join us tonight."

Anybody who pushes you beyond that point deserves a plain no. If other people flatly refuse to be nice, you have no obligation to let them coerce you into something you don't want to do.

An adult party is an adult party. Nice people always have the right to say, "No children allowed." For that reason, kids should never be taken along when they're not invited. But if somebody does that to you, always remember that it's your territory. The ball is in your court.

12

The Mouth
of the Gift Horse

The giving and receiving of presents ought to be one of life's particular joys. For that reason, it may not seem a subject that should present any major problems, one that is more a matter of going along with traditional "etiquette" than anything else. But I have found that it's an area in which nice people are constantly coming to grief, finding themselves offended, or wondering how in the world they ought to react.

We're not talking here about the niceties of writing thank-you notes for wedding gifts, or any of those questions of pure "etiquette." There are plenty of books and newspaper columns dealing with that side of things. I want to look instead at the psychology of giving—and of receiving.

There are all kinds of gifts, from jars of homemade jelly to rare books, from a souvenir trinket picked up on a trip to Mexico to a case of fine California Burgundy. When you are taken to the theater or out to dinner, you are receiving a gift. There are chintzy gifts, joke gifts, self-aggrandizing gifts, overgenerous gifts, and considerate gifts. In both the giving and receiving of gifts, however, the nature of the gift in and of itself is not as important as the context in which it is given and the spirit of the giver.

There are people who expect gifts, and those who resent them. There are people who feel that a gift must always be reciprocated in turn, and others who feel no such compunction. People who expect gifts will be offended if they don't receive them, those who resent them will be annoyed if they do. People who feel they have to return the favor may be embarrassed by the lavishness of a gift, while people of the opposite persuasion may irritate the giver.

It is no small task for the nice person to keep all these subtleties straight, because the right thing to do and the right way to react changes from person to person and situation to situation. Let's look at those subtleties in three areas:

1. Responding to the chintzy and the overgenerous gift.
2. What to do when guests bring edible gifts to parties.
3. Fighting over the dinner check.

Tightwads and Self-Aggrandizers

The world is full of people who regard themselves as frugal but whom other people see as tightwads. It's this difference in perception between the giver and the receiver that causes all the trouble. The presents one gives, after all, are a projection of one's self-image. Very frugal people may feel that they've been generous by giving anything at all, no matter how chintzy, and will expect effusive thanks for what may be a mere token. The recipients, however, may be hard put to wax enthusiastic over what they regard as a piece of garbage.

A friend of mine, whom I'll call Joan, has a particularly keen awareness of the degree to which gifts are an expression of self-image. Joan has a child the same age as my Elizabeth, and we live in the same neighborhood. Following Elizabeth's sixth birthday party, Joan was helping me clean up; as she did so, she began looking over the presents Elizabeth had received, about twenty of them, which were laid out on a side table. Without seeing any of the cards, she began to identify which present had been brought by which neighborhood child, making her judgment on the basis of her knowledge of the various mothers involved.

The first one was easy. "That's Regina Huddlestone at work," she said, pointing to an art gum eraser in the shape of an automobile. "I know because one of my kids got exactly the same thing three months ago. I'll bet Regina picked up a dozen of them for ten bucks and will be passing them out for months."

Many of the other presents were much more expensive items, and didn't duplicate anything Joan's kids had received, yet she went on to match the gift with the giver correctly in all but two cases. She told me that the criteria she used were how expensive the gift was, the kind of taste it reflected and, in a few cases, how imaginative it was.

In light of the cheapness of the art gum eraser, I asked Joan what she was planning to buy for Regina's daughter, whose birthday was coming up. "Well, there are two temptations," Joan said. "The first is to give something equally chintzy. The second is to give something that's clearly expensive, in order to embarrass Regina. The trouble is, I don't think Regina is embarrassable on that score. You also have to remember that the present is for the kid, and she'd be disappointed in some piece of junk. So I'm going to opt for the middle course and buy something very cute but only moderately expensive."

Joan's solution to this problem seems to me both the most sensible and the nicest one available. The reasoning behind it also seems to me a fine example of the way a nice person has to think through such situations, taking the context fully into account. As I discussed in chapter 11, it's not fair to take out on kids the failures of their parents.

In terms of reciprocal gift-giving between adults, things can get trickier. While as a general rule it can be said that one should try to keep things in balance, there are exceptions, and it is the exceptions that tell the real story. For instance, every Christmas your Aunt Martha sends you a five-dollar cotton wall-hanging with a sentimental illustration and the twelve months of the year in calendar form. There really isn't space for it in your kitchen, you can't write on it, and it's not especially to your taste. It goes in a drawer. You, on the other hand, send Aunt Martha a rather expensive full year membership in a "club" that ships out fruit or boxes of variegated edible goodies. And there's a reason for the discrepancy in the nature and money value of the gifts. Aunt Martha is living on Social Security and a small pension. She can't do very much in the way of gift-giving, but she tries. What's more, you realize that, for her, being able to send even the smallest token is a form of personal reassurance— it makes her feel better about herself. You could tell her to save the money and spend it on herself, but she would be hurt. Also, the fact that she has sent *something* to you makes it easier to accept the out-of-season fruit or special delicacies that she dotes on but could never afford to buy for herself. In other words, there is a tacit understanding between you that makes for a legitimate and rather touching compact, regardless of how unbalanced it is in purely material terms.

On the other side of the coin, unfortunately, we have the can-you-top-this gift givers. No matter what you give them on one occasion, they'll come back next time around with something more glamorous, unusual, or expensive. Never allow yourself to become involved in this kind of contest. Just keep right on giving the kind and value of gift you felt was appropriate to the relationship in the first place—unless, of course, something drastic happens to the relationship like getting married. By maintaining your own equilibrium in such cases, you will quickly find out whether the other person or couple simply enjoys giving terrific presents, regardless of what they get in return, or whether they are in fact playing a very materialistic game. If they keep on giving you expensive presents, fine, you've established a compact like the one you have with Aunt Martha. If they start pulling back a notch, and then two or three, you will know that their real object was the game of proving to you that they had better taste and/or more money than you do. And you will have in fact won the game, even if in an upside-down fashion.

The nice person understands, indeed, that the overgenerous gift can cause the recipient embarrassment or even arouse resentment. A young couple I know told me a story that illustrates the pain that can be inflicted by someone who behaves in an overgenerous way. Brian and Carole had been riding high for four or five years. In their early thirties, they'd achieved at least a strong start toward the kind of success they wanted for themselves, Brian in advertising and Carole as a painter. Brian's company went bankrupt, it seemed overnight, and while their combined incomes had allowed them to live very well, they suddenly found themselves living on less than half as much.

Brian and Carole had always been sentimental about Christmas, and made a great deal of it, giving a large Christmas party, with presents for everyone who came. This year there would be no Christmas party, and they planned to give one another only one or two very practical gifts. One of their closest friends, a woman they'd both known since college, decided to take up the slack. During the week before Christmas, she arrived at their apartment almost every day bearing a shopping bag full of gifts, large and small, and all for them. No doubt she was trying to be nice, trying to show that she cared, but with each visit they became more and more depressed and, in the end, angry. Their friend's generosity was merely serving to emphasize the plight they found themselves in, and to make them feel guilty because they could barely reciprocate at all. It was a case of generosity run amok.

The nice person must always keep in mind that there is a point beyond which giving becomes a kind of assault.

I Knew You Could Use It

One summer, Joe and I gave a large buffet garden party on a Sunday afternoon. About half an hour after the party had begun, a couple arrived with a present for us, a surprise. A surprise it certainly was—a smoked bluefish almost a yard in length. "With all these people," said the wife, "I knew you could use it."

"How spectacular," I said, "But I don't know what we'll put it on."

"Oh, we'll find something," she replied. And so a search was begun for an oversize platter. In the back of the pantry one was finally uncovered, cracked but usable. But of course it had to be washed. Meanwhile, I was contemplating which of the dishes we had prepared ourselves would have to be swept to the grass from the already overladen buffet tables to accommodate this outsize aquatic intruder.

I started to leave the kitchen to survey the tables to see what could be removed, but was caught up sharply by another request. "I didn't get around to making the sauce. Do you have, let's see, sour cream, horseradish . . ."

Another search was begun. But I excused myself from this one. "I'm sure you'll find everything you need somewhere.

That's the spice cabinet, and just go ahead and rummage through the refrigerator. I've really got to get back to the rest of our guests."

The bluefish, eventually, turned out to be delicious. Having deprived me of nearly twenty minutes of mingling with my guests, it had an obligation to be.

People who take presents of food and wine to other people's parties are trying to be nice. At least some of them are—we'll get to that question in a moment. But they drive me crazy. It's my party. I have decided on a menu, chosen the wines, worked hard to see to it that everything is just right. I don't need and don't want somebody else's contributions, no matter how delicious. And they are not, by the way, always delicious.

Of course, if you're having a potluck dinner, which is becoming more common these days, that's fine. Everybody knows what they're supposed to contribute, and if someone brings along a little extra something it isn't going to make any difference since the feast is bound to be a fairly eclectic one to begin with. But if people bring along unannounced edible gifts to a party that is yours alone—or worse, having asked if they can bring something and been told no, bring it anyway—you have every right to want to upend their offering over their heads.

You can't do that, unfortunately. Nice people don't get into foodfights except in very special circumstances. (When Joe and I were "courting" I did once overturn a platter of Italian pastry on him, leaving him covered with powdered sugar, and he retaliated a few days later at a resort hotel where we'd gone to make up, by shoving a Boston cream pie in my face as I walked out of the bathroom freshly showered. But that's another story.) You can't do that kind of thing to mere friends who are visiting in your home. The sad fact is that you can't do much of anything.

If you don't serve the dish, the person who brought it will undoubtedly be mortally offended and will certainly bring the missing highlight of the meal to everyone else's attention. You can, however, at least protect your own culinary reputation by making sure to carry the dish in yourself, separately, and announce in a loud voice, "Oh, look what Natalie brought." Natalie will be pleased beyond words, but the other guests will get the point: this one ain't mine, kids, do what you will with it.

Wine is a little easier to handle. When someone arrives with a bottle of wine and says, "You should open it right away, to let it breathe," or, "I think it may need a little more chilling," you've got an out. I say, or Joe says, "Well, we've got a wine we particularly want you to try. Do you mind if we save this for next time you come? That way we can plan a meal around it." Mind you, if what your guest has brought is far superior to what you were planning to serve, and it goes with the meal, by all means serve it. But don't let yourself forget that you've just been one-upped.

That brings us back to the question of whether people who bring unannounced edibles and insist that they be served forthwith are really being so nice. Some innocents may indeed be, but a lot of people who do this are really trying to upstage you. You can tell by the way they feast on any compliment thrown their way, or hover around the buffet table identifying their handiwork to all and sundry.

This is not to say that the nice person doesn't bring presents of food or wine to a party. A great many nice people do. But they *present* it to you in a certain way. I have a dear friend, Trixie Burke, who's a marvelous cook, and who always brings something to eat when invited to our house. It's always beautifully laid out in a wicker basket or tied up with ribbons. And she brings it on into the kitchen, sets it down on the table, and says, "I brought a little something. You can use it tonight if you want to, but you might want to save it for yourselves."

Now that's a nice person and a lovely present.

Let Me Get That

Perhaps because it doesn't come gift wrapped, the act of taking someone out to dinner at a restaurant is not always fully understood to be what it actually is: a form of present. We all understand it in certain circumstances, of course. The wedding anniversary dinner at a restaurant favored in premarital days, the Mother's Day excursion to a country inn, the announced birthday present of a night on the town—in these contexts everyone recognizes that the "treat" is in fact a gift.

But things get muddled in the ordinary course of life, especially when the people involved dine out together fairly regularly. At the backs of their minds, people are obviously aware that in deciding who's going to pick up the check the real issue is who's going to give who a present this time, but all too often that awareness translates itself into a kind of contest that no one at the table would dream of getting involved in if they were dealing with cashmere sweaters, crystal ashtrays, or copper mixing bowls.

Here again we find ourselves in that dangerous territory between the Scylla and Charybdis of tightwaddery and self-aggrandizement. In this instance, self-aggrandizement, in the form of always insisting on paying the check, leads to the more violent public display, with people raising their voices to utter an intimidating, "Absolutely not, I said I'm getting it," or knocking over water glasses to grab the check out of one another's hands. In either case, it is a distasteful way to end a social occasion.

The tightwad, of course, is absolutely silent. Some people who never pay the check are basically social gigolos; their charm, wit, or beauty, real or imagined, is such that they expect to be "taken care of" for the privilege of their company. So long as the person who's paying is happy to agree, there can be no faulting this arrangement—a compact has been entered into, a tawdry compact in some cases, but a compact nevertheless.

But most people who never pay the check are more likely to be examples of why the rich get richer. They could well afford to do so; they're just plain tight with their money. Short of asking them point blank why they never pay the check, which would be rude, or announcing that one is short of cash, which would be self-abasing, the only real alternative is to let the check lie there. And lie there, and lie there. Sometimes it actually works. I think the real answer to this situation, though, after you've paid the check a half-dozen times in a row, is to ask yourself a simple question: "Why am I friends with this person, anyway?" If you can come up with a good answer, then you've got yourself an unspoken contract and you might as well just go on paying the check. Otherwise, you'd do well to take a close look at chapter 7, in terms of how to end a friendship.

The true expense account luncheon is to some extent a different matter. There may still be a contest as to who will pay the check, but since the company rather than the individual is really paying, this becomes a form of professional gamesmanship and belongs in a different category. It has to do with business status, which quite often has absolutely nothing to do with being a nice person. It should, and it can, but it often doesn't.

On the other hand, many nice people misunderstand the lengths to which expense accounts can be stretched. I have a woman friend with whom I lunch occasionally simply as a friend. She is the wife of a very wealthy lawyer, and is perfectly content to raise their three children rather than pursue a career. When we had lunch no business was discussed, and there was no way I could justify billing such a social occasion to CBS. Yet she always let me pay the bill. I realized that she *thought* I was charging the meals to my expense account, and therefore saw no reason to offer to pay. I didn't want to explain the situation too bluntly, so at one luncheon I pulled out my corporate American Express card, started to put it down and said, "Whoops, wrong card. Where's my personal one?" I then fished around and took out my personal card.

Nice people know how to take a hint, and my friend immediately said, "Pat, have you been paying for all our lunches yourself?"

I replied, "Well, you have to be very careful with expense accounts these days. Don't worry about it."

"Nonsense, I'm sorry for being so dim. This one's on me, and so are the next few."

Now, when we lunch, we alternate treating one another. For people who eat out regularly together, I think that alternating the picking up of the check is by far the most sensible and pleasant way to deal with the matter. If people are living on a tight budget, the "Dutch treat" approach is of course more practical. But while the Dutch treat works well enough when only two people are involved, it can get terribly messy if there are four or more, degenerating into the "everyone who had tomato juice raise his hand" syndrome. For many years, my mother lunched regularly with the same group of women, and she often came away annoyed because the check got divided up wrong. I finally persuaded her that instead of squabbling among themselves over two-dollar differentials, it would be much nicer if each woman took turns paying the entire bill—over the course of a year, it was bound to even out. I do have one caveat to that advice, however: people who have extra drinks from the bar should chip in some extra cash to cover them.

Taking friends out to dine is a form of gift-giving. The best way to prevent such occasions from becoming a contest, or collapsing into squabbles, is to make sure that everyone involved is aware of the compact you have formed ahead of time. It's all too easy for even nice people to get into a snit over their after-dinner coffee.

13

Money, Money, Money, or Polonius Was Right

"Money," as the John Kander and Fred Ebb song from *Cabaret* so succinctly puts it, "makes the world go round." Unfortunately, it can also make the world go sour. Money is something that a great many people find it hard to be nice about. Some people think about money too much, and some think about it too little. There are people who try to impress you with how much money they have, and desire your envy. There are people who seem to have forgotten the value of a dollar, and put you in the position of shelling out more than you can afford. And then there is the tricky matter of borrowing and lending.

I've touched on money matters several times in this book —it's a subject that comes up in many different contexts— but there remains a lot to be said. I'd like to discuss being nice about money in three major areas:

1. How to deal with people who want to spend your money their way.

2. How to handle borrowing and lending.
3. How to deal with financial show-offs.

If We Just All Chip In

When I was fresh out of college I was asked to be a bridesmaid at the wedding of a very wealthy college friend. I accepted happily. But then I discovered that I'd gotten myself
into a situation that created real problems for me. In addition
to travel expenses and the cost of the bridesmaid's dress,
which I was prepared for, I found that I was also expected
to chip in for a wedding present that was to be a collective
offering of the entire wedding party. It was a spectacular
present, an antique Georgian silver punch bowl, accompanied
by twenty-four silver mugs; each mug was to be engraved
with the name of a member of the wedding party or close
friend who had contributed to the cost of the gift. That cost
was $12,000, or $500 per person. That was a lot of money
for me. I was about to spend several months studying in
Mexico, and every dollar counted. Five hundred dollars, in
those days, was the equivalent of almost two months of living
expenses in Mexico.

I paid my share, but I wasn't at all happy about it. I considered saying that I simply couldn't afford to give that much,
but that would have meant that someone else, or several people, would have had to make up the difference, and I didn't
feel right about that even though any number of people in
the wedding party could have put in an extra hundred dollars
or so without even blinking. What should have happened, of
course, is that the members of the wedding party should have
been told what the present cost and asked to give what they
could toward it, with the wealthier participants taking up the
slack. That would have been the nice way to handle it. But
I'm sure it simply never occurred to anyone. People who have

money often tend to lose sight of the fact that a mere $500 to them is a small fortune to many other people.

Now, you obviously aren't going to be asked to contribute to the purchase of antique silver punch bowls very often. But you can be sure you'll be asked to shell out ten bucks, or twenty-five, or fifty every so often to help buy a group present for somebody's birthday, or shower, or retirement party. That goes on in practically every office building on the continent all the time. And it's my strong opinion that the nice person has no obligation to contribute. For one thing, it's a way of spending your money for you; you're being told how much to put into the pot. For another thing, you can be certain that the person whose idea it is is going to make sure the recipient knows that—in other words, the "organizer" is going to get the bulk of the credit. I say that if that person wants the credit for giving an expensive gift, let him or her buy it and pay for it alone.

Of course, it's hard to refuse to contribute to a group gift of this kind. Essentially, your being blackmailed. If you don't contribute, your name won't go on the card, and everyone in the office, especially the recipient of the present, is going to think you're a mean-spirited cheapskate. That's a good reason in itself to refuse, I think, unless you have some masochistic desire to be blackmailed.

In fact, you're probably going to *have* to give a present. But make it your own present. When you're asked to contribute, say, "Oh, I'd love to, but the thing is that I've already bought Susan a lovely little vase." Then go buy a lovely little vase. You will be spending your money as you see fit, and buying something that reflects your taste and not somebody else's. This ploy has the additional advantage of putting a crimp in the "organizer's" plan to hog the credit.

There are a lot of organizers around who seem to spend a good deal of time thinking up new and creative ways to spend other people's money. They suggest giving a joint party

—at your house. They suggest an evening on the town—they'll get the theater tickets, and you can take care of the restaurant, the only problem being that they know *just* the restaurant, and it turns out to cost twenty-five dollars more per person than the price of the theater tickets. They suggest it would save everybody money if you drove only one car to work, except that it turns out to be your car, and although they grandly pay the fifty-cent toll on the highway, you're stuck with the bill for gas.

Don't let them do it to you. Nice people often tend to get squeamish when it comes to asking other people to pay their fair share. This is an area in which I think we all have to toughen up a little and remember that it's only a short step from being a nice person to being a sucker.

The best defense against being turned into a sucker is the simple word "we." "Shall *we* split the bill?" "Shall *we* stop for gas?" "Why don't *we* both keep an accounting, so we don't get confused." We is a wonderfully inclusive little word, and by getting in the habit of using it regularly, the nice person can avoid a lot of mooching and the misunderstandings that go with it. There's another word worth making a habitual part of your vocabulary when dealing with people who want to spend your money their way. The word is *share,* as in, "Your *share* comes to," or "Shall we *share* expenses?"

Since nice people are always the first to share their bounty, they should never be afraid to ask others to share the burden.

The Small-Change Artist

I am constantly amazed at the number of people who never seem to have enough cash on them to take care of utterly predictable daily needs like lunch or taxi fare home. I'm not talking about the unemployed, or young actors and writers who can barely pay the rent, or panhandlers who are trying to put together enough cup-of-coffee quarters to buy another pint of Ripple. I'm talking about men in pin-striped suits and women with Gucci handbags who never seem to have a dime in their pockets and are always having to borrow ten dollars until tomorrow.

Maybe it's just a reflection of our credit card economy in which pieces of plastic have come to seem more real than dollar bills, but I suspect that there are more complicated and more individualistic reasons why so many well-paid professionals, or even very wealthy tycoons and magnates, wander through life borrowing small sums at every turn. Both John F. Kennedy and Nelson Rockefeller, for example, were famous for it, cadging five dollars here and ten dollars there from their aides, Secret Service men, and even reporters, almost none of whom apparently ever saw the money again. Perhaps five dollars was such a negligible sum to these multimillionaires that it simply never occurred to them that it meant a movie ticket, a couple of drinks, or a steak sandwich to the ordinary mortals they borrowed from. But then again, there are ordinary mortals who behave the same way.

Whatever the psychological mysteries involved, I don't think nice people have to put up with these "small-change artists," especially the ones who forget to repay you. I don't mind in the least lending a few dollars to someone who doesn't ask too often and who I know will repay it the next morning. But with people who are constantly "out of pocket," I think the nice person has every right to say, "I'm short myself," or "I haven't been to the bank today," or "I'm afraid I'm going to need all my cash myself." Why should you have to make an extra trip to the bank because someone else is too lazy or disorganized to do it himself or herself?

If you have lent someone ten dollars and he or she forgets to repay you—and in most cases such people really do forget

—should you just let it go? Undoubtedly, that's the nicest thing to do, but in my opinion it's also foolhardy. Nice people shouldn't confuse themselves with savings and loan institutions. Of course, if you've only lent someone bus fare, it becomes a different matter—the nice person doesn't make an issue over nickels and dimes. If you do decide to try to collect, I think the direct but casual approach is best: "Do you happen to have that ten dollars I lent you last week?" Some people prefer to pretend that *they've* lost track, and say, "I'm confused. Did you pay me back that ten dollars?" On the surface, this latter approach sounds nicer, but most people are going to take it as insincere, knowing full well that you're not in the least confused. On balance, direct is better.

When dealing with someone who's constantly "letting" you pick up the tab, I believe it's necessary to let them know what they're doing—because often they aren't fully aware of the cadging habit they've developed. A former colleague of mine, a male reporter, never seemed to have any money on him, especially when he was in taxis. He'd hail the cab and you'd jump in together, and then when you reached your destination, he'd look in his wallet and say, "Sorry, Pat, can you get this one?" After numerous "this ones," I finally said to him, "You know, Steve, one of these days neither of us is going to have any money on us and some cabby is going to call the cops." He was better about it after that—not perfect, but better.

And then there are the women, and men, who ask if they can put a purchase on your credit card. They don't have an account at the store you're shopping in, or have forgotten their credit card, and they've just seen the perfect blouse for themselves, or the perfect bauble for the wife's birthday. The nice person who asks you to put the purchase on your credit card will send you a check for the amount the next day, but since you can't count on that happening, I think it's wise to say, "Oh, sure. When the bill comes in I'll send you a copy of it for your files." That's protecting yourself up front, so that if you aren't repaid quickly, you can send them a copy of the bill without it coming across like a dunning notice.

It may be hard to say no to small-change artists, but that doesn't mean allowing yourself to be turned into a sucker.

Serious Money

In terms of lending larger amounts of money—two hundred, a thousand, two thousand dollars—whether to a friend or a relative, Polonius's advice from *Hamlet* still applies: "Neither a borrower nor a lender be; for loan oft loses both itself and friend."

There are times when someone close to us really needs financial help, and the nice person is going to come to the rescue in an emergency if he or she can afford it. But by afford it, I mean afford to give the money away, not loan it. As a general rule, the larger the sum of money you lend on a personal basis, the less likely you are to get it back. If you are going to lend someone serious money, I think it's vital to look upon it in your own mind as a gift. That way, if you don't get it back, you won't lose the friend as well as the loan. If you do get it back you can take pleasure in a nice surprise. I wouldn't tell the person it's a gift, unless it actually is, but that is the assumption you should make privately. Otherwise, I wouldn't make the loan in the first place.

Don't loan serious money if you can't afford to kiss it goodbye for good.

Life Among the Nouveaux Riches

There are people who want to spend your money their way. There are people who want to borrow money from you. In both cases, you're being asked to part with hard cash. Yet one of the curious things about money is that we can be made to feel badly about it without spending a cent. There are a lot of people out there with a genius for putting other people down in monetary terms.

Let me give you an example. There were two men in their early forties who had grown up together on the same block in New York City's Coney Island. I'll call them David and Martin. Their hard-working blue-collar families managed to send both David and Martin to fine colleges. David went on to become a professor of English, while Martin became a stockbroker.

Martin, who by now was a very wealthy man, invited David to lunch while David was visiting New York following the publication of a novel he'd written about his Coney Island boyhood. The novel had received rave reviews, crept onto the bestseller lists for two or three weeks, and had been optioned for a movie.

"I hope you made some money out of the book," Martin said over lunch.

"Some," said David. "But I squandered half what's come in so far on a new BMW."

"Great little car," replied Martin. "I gave my daughter one for her sixteenth birthday."

A great little car! To David, his BMW was a prized possession he had never been able to afford in the past. To Martin it was a present suitable to a teenager. And by announcing that, Martin was putting David very thoroughly in his place. That may not have been his intention, but it was certainly the effect.

It has been my observation over the years that people like Martin simply can't help themselves—they are so proud of their own financial success that they have just got to make sure that everyone else is impressed too. People who have grown up with a lot of money can take it for granted in ways that lead to insensitivity toward people who know the real meaning of a hard-won dollar—as with my friends who expected me to contribute a full share to the silver punch bowl. But at least they don't usually spend all their time trying to impress you with how much money they have—in fact they often try to disguise the extent of their wealth. It is the nouveaux riches, the Martins of this world, who show off their success at every turn, putting down other people in the process.

In dealing with such people, the nice person has the right to retaliate. Subtlety, I might add, will get you nowhere. For example, when David was told that Martin had given his daughter a BMW for her sixteenth birthday, he replied drily, "Well, that's one way to learn how to drive." That passed right over Martin's head, and had no impact whatsoever. Forget the dry wit. What Martin has to be made to understand, at least glimmeringly, is that he's being offensive. I would have said something like, "I suppose that means she'll get a Rolls-Royce for her twenty-first birthday. If I write a couple more best-sellers, I might even be able to afford one for myself by then."

Since financial show-offs think of everything in terms of money, you can only get through to them by putting things in strictly monetary perspective. A few years ago, a newly rich neighbor of ours bought a co-op Joe and I had looked at but decided we didn't much like. The man told Joe, "I just bought that co-op you were thinking about. Eight hundred thousand." What he was saying, of course, was that we obviously couldn't afford such an apartment but that he could. Joe had the perfect comeback for that one. "Good for you," he said. "That's almost exactly twice what we could have had it for."

I was once at a party where a woman complimented the hostess on the caviar being served as a first course. The hostess replied, "It should be good at thirty dollars an ounce."

"Mercy," the first woman said, without losing a beat, "you mean I just ate a fifty-dollar bill?"

Most of us, though, can't think that fast. And the question arises as to whether it's worth the effort to always try to reply in kind to financial show-offs. If you aren't careful, you can get a reputation for having an acid tongue, which isn't exactly the hallmark of the nice person. I think the occasional retaliatory comment is perfectly in order, but the nice person shouldn't make a habit of it. Sometimes it's better to just let it go. For example, when a guest says, "Oh, I just love this china. It's what we use at our *summer* place," I think it's hardly worthwhile to try to respond to the implication that they use something much *better* in the city. I'd just smile and say, "Isn't it nice we all have such good taste." Part of being a nice person, after all, is feeling secure enough not to take offense when someone else is behaving badly toward you.

14

The Customer
Is Always Right

Your best suit has come back from the cleaners with half the buttons missing. You are having a business lunch at an expensive restaurant and not only is the service slow, but your steak arrives well done instead of medium rare, there are rolls but no butter on the table, your guest's side order of creamed spinach never arrives, and there is almost as much coffee in the saucer as in the cup. You've left your car overnight for a minor repair job, but the mechanic has managed to find several other bugs for which you are being charged an extra $90; what's more, there now seems to be a problem with the brakes that didn't exist before. A department store delivers the wrong sofa two weeks late, and your bank has "misplaced" a transfer from your savings account to your checking account with the result that checks are bouncing like tennis balls.

You're angry.

And you have every right to be. To make matters worse, the cleaner, the waiter, and the auto mechanic are probably going to insist that it's not their problem. Instead of the customer always being right—the theory on which American commerce was built—the customer these days is usually informed that he or she is being unreasonable.

You want to scream.

Don't. It's bad for the blood pressure and more often than not it will get you nowhere at all. It will in fact only fortify most incompetents in their belief that you're just a troublemaker.

So what is the nice person to do? Should you simply swallow your anger and retreat?

Not at all.

To begin with, the nice person can take a leaf from the handbook of many politicians: Don't Get Mad, Get Even. In stores and restaurants, the best way to get even is to walk out. But it's important to make a point to the management in the way you walk out. You're not going to get even simply by disappearing into the street. You should make it clear why you are walking out. That can be done without raising your voice and it can be done with complete dignity, as we'll see.

In many other cases, however, you'll find yourself dealing with a situation after the fact, and be forced to do it by letter or over the telephone. The undelivered sofa, the messed-up bank account, the computer error on your credit card bill—these situations require a different approach. And it is here that being nice, behaving politely and calmly, can serve as one of your most effective tools in getting the matter taken care of promptly.

Let's look at these situations in more detail, to see how you can:

1. Get even, with dignity, on the spot.
2. Use simple niceness as a tool for dealing with company representatives over the telephone.

Exit to Applause

My husband has little tolerance for incompetence. But he also has a sense of humor and an ingenious turn of mind. Joe is one of those people who usually thinks of the perfect comeback right at the moment, instead of hours afterward. That can be annoying when I'm on one side of a debate and he's on the other, but in general it's an ability I envy. He put it to especially good use one Saturday afternoon in a sporting goods store.

He'd picked out a variety of items for the family, from sweat socks to lifejackets, about $75 worth of merchandise. It was a big sporting goods store with checkout counters, but only one cash register was open, perhaps because it was lunchtime. The cash register was computerized, the check-out clerk was not. The total came to $175 and change. Obviously the check-out clerk had added an extra zero to some $10 item.

"I'm afraid you've made a mistake, Miss," Joe said.

"No, Sir," the check-out clerk replied. "These registers don't make mistakes. They're computerized. If that's what the total says, it's right."

"Computers do in fact break down," Joe replied, reasonably. "But in this case I think the mistake is yours. You must have punched in an extra zero someplace. It should be about $75, not $175."

"See what it says, Sir? That's what you owe."

By this time there were four more people in line behind Joe. Groans were heard. The woman right behind Joe, in an exasperated tone, said, "I think the gentleman is right, Miss. Why don't you just do it over again. You have a lot of people waiting on line here."

"I can't do it over, it will throw the totals off."

"The totals are already off," Joe said with some asperity. "Why don't you call the manager and let him straighten it out?"

"I don't need the manager, Sir, unless you continue to be so difficult. Do you want to pay for these things or not?"

"You know, I don't think I do," Joe replied. "Of course that will throw your totals off, too, won't it?"

"Yes, it will, Sir. Thanks a lot."

"Miss, will you just get on with it," a man farther back in the line called out loudly. "What's your problem anyway?"

Joe paused for a moment. "Okay look, I've decided I don't really need these things." He turned to the woman behind him. "Do you really want to buy these items today?"

The woman looked a bit startled but then smiled and said, "I'm beginning to wonder."

"May I have them?" Joe asked.

"What are you going to do with them?"

"Teach a little lesson."

"Take them," she said.

All but one of the people in line surrendered their merchandise to Joe. The exception was a man with two cans of tennis balls. "I'm sorry," he said. "But my wife would kill me. Mixed doubles, you know."

His arms laden, Joe marched to the back of the store where a middle-aged man was overseeing a stock boy. "Are you the manager?" Joe asked.

The people from the line had followed Joe, and were hovering at a discreet distance.

"Yes, I'm the manager."

Joe set his burden down in a heap at the manager's feet. "I figure that there's about six hundred dollars' worth of stuff here that you could have sold to all these people if you had more than one cash register open or trained your checkout personnel properly. Sorry about that."

The audience of customers broke into applause, including

the man with the tennis balls, who said, "Here, you'd better take these, too. My wife will love this story."

And they all walked out of the store together.

Not all of us, of course, would have the nerve to play the pied piper the way Joe did in this case. But when you run into situations of this sort, it's always possible to do the same thing on an individual basis. Don't just leave your merchandise on the counter with the check-out person or the salesperson, though. Go find the manager. If you just walk out and write a letter later, it will have no effect whatsoever. Letters can easily be ignored altogether, thrown in the wastebasket or, at best, answered with a form letter that doesn't begin to acknowledge the specific circumstances. All too many businesses these days seem to have adopted the attitude that only cranks write letters of complaint, and they treat such communications with barely disguised contempt.

When you wheel your cart full of groceries up to the supermarket manager, or carry an armful of clothes over to the floor manager of a department store and announce, "Will you take charge of these, please. I don't have the time to wait any longer to pay for them," that individual will almost always try to mollify you and make the sale. The supermarket manager may offer to open up another cash register himself to take care of you, the floor manager may guide you over to a salesperson and tell them to take care of you immediately. Don't be tempted. First of all, you've made a rather grand gesture, and grand gestures should never be interrupted midway. Like the very heavy opera singer of a generation ago who, playing Tosca at the Metropolitan Opera, leaped over the parapet to her death, hit the backstage net and bounced back into view in a horizontal position, the grand gesture that is taken back is likely to invite ridicule.

What's more, you will only succeed in infuriating other customers who have also been waiting in line or desperately trying to get a salesperson's attention themselves. You're just inviting murmured imprecations, audible inquiries as to who the hell you think you are, or an angry, "Hey, lady, you were behind me." There is a very famous Broadway musical star who is under the distinct impression that she owns New York, and she never waits in line for anything. Whether she's going to the movies or buying tissues at the corner drugstore, she simply sweeps past everyone and demands immediate attention. She is not well liked. Nice people do not jump lines, and you should never allow yourself to be tempted by a store manager who offers you that privilege. Your object in approaching the manager in the first place was to make it clear that the store or department is badly run; the technique shouldn't be used as a ploy to get special favors.

The same rule applies in restaurants, which *I* sometimes walk out of. Restaurants should be treated like full professors, many of whom are notorious for showing up a half-hour late or not at all for classes they are teaching reluctantly. When I was in college, the rule was that you gave the full professor twenty minutes to show up; after that I left. In restaurants, if I haven't been able to get a waiter's attention after twenty minutes, I leave. I don't care how expensive and chic the restaurant is. They took my reservation, for a specified time. I'm not interested in such excuses as, "We have a waiter out sick," or "The chef is in a bad mood today." At an expensive restaurant, one is paying extra for service and consistency of performance. If the restaurant can't deliver, that's their problem. At a business lunch, it doesn't bother me for a moment to say to my guest, no matter how important he or she may be, "This is a waste of time, let's go across the street to the deli, get a couple of sandwiches, and take them back to my office." I've never had anyone object to that solution.

But walking out of a restaurant is again a grand gesture. The maître d' will more than likely try to waylay you, with promises of instant service. After all, having customers walk out is embarrassing; it's certain to make diners at adjacent tables wonder if they shouldn't have done the same thing. But don't allow yourself to be coaxed into returning to your table. For one thing, in order to provide you with instant service, your waiter is going to have to neglect other tables—it's the "who the hell is she" syndrome again. What's more, the maître d' will undoubtedly scold the waiter, who is going to resent you as a result—he may put on a burst of speed, but graciousness should not be expected. The chef, especially if he is in a bad mood to begin with, will not appreciate being told that your orders have priority, and dishes may well arrive at your table barely tepid, or scorched, or you may be treated to the stringiest steak or stalest shrimp he can rustle up.

When a maître d' tries to persuade me to stay, whether I've been sitting at a table or held at the bar waiting to be seated, I smile and say, "You seem to be overbooked today, and we really don't have the time. Thank you anyway."

The "thank you anyway," is important, giving you the final, polite word. It also holds out the vague hope that you might return another time, cutting off any remarks about people who make reservations and don't honor them.

The nice person has the perfect right to take a hike, but there is no need to raise one's voice or make unpleasant remarks. The walking out, in and of itself, will get the message across, and leave you with the feeling of having handled the situation with dignity and calm.

Hold, Please

Making your displeasure known in person, on the spot, has definite advantages in many ways. It's always easier to keep control of a dispute if you can look the other person in the eye. You can give a slight smile to mitigate the rather tough tone of voice you've adopted. Facial expressions, gestures, and body language can be used to get across your feelings. But in many cases, the angry consumer is faced with the necessity of getting action over the telephone.

Like most people, I have a love/hate relationship with the telephone. It makes life much easier in a great many ways, but it also has a large number of built-in frustrations and irritations connected with it. For the angry consumer trying to get through to a department store, credit card company, bank or power company to complain about unde-livered merchandise, incorrect bills or statements, the frustra-tions can outweight the convenience. All the circuits may be busy for half an hour at a time. When you do get through you may find yourself put on hold for several minutes while being regaled, appropriately enough, with a Mantovani rendi-tion of "The Impossible Dream." The chances of your getting cut off are extremely high, especially if you're annoyed to begin with. Thus, by the time you've actually established contact with another human being, you may be ready to spit nails.

But it's essential to get a grip on yourself. You have to remember that the individual who takes your call is in fact a person doing a job, and that the problem you've encountered isn't *their* fault. Somebody else made the mistake. What's more, the person you're talking to has been dealing with a lot of other complaints. (In fact, I try to make such calls in the morning, when the company representative is likely to be in a better mood than at the end of the day.)

Remembering that I'm talking to a *person,* I always start by saying, "Good morning," or "Good afternoon." This is such a ritualistic phrase, uttered so many times in the course of a day, that it can usually be gotten out in a fairly even voice no matter how upset you may be. Simply saying it is likely to have a calming effect on you. Even more important, it predisposes the representatives you've reached to relax a little themselves. Their first thought isn't going to be, "Oh

God, this one's going to be nasty," but rather, "This one sounds civilized." People who take calls from the public, which are more than likely to be complaints, have defenses. They *must* have defenses or they'd go crazy. By starting off politely, giving the impression that you're a nice person, you give yourself an edge, making it possible to penetrate the representative's defenses at least slightly.

The next things to say is: "I'm afraid I have a problem." The word "afraid" in that sentence further suggests that you're a nice person, and indicates that you realize the person you are talking to isn't personally responsible. Then give as clear and simple an explanation of your problem as possible. You don't need to inform them that the company they work for is run by a bunch of crooks or incompetents. They know all about incompetence; the reason they have their jobs taking calls from customers is that things go wrong, on a regular basis.

Sometimes your problem can be cleared up immediately. But more often you may be asked to send a canceled check to prove that your bill has in fact been paid, be told that the matter will have to be checked into, or promised that your new refrigerator wasn't delivered as scheduled because the truck broke down and will be arriving tomorrow.

Delays. More frustration.

But this is not the time to blow your top. You've built up some good will by being polite and calm. Don't spoil things by concluding your conversation with an angry remark. If it's a matter of a delayed delivery, it's fine to point out that you've already stayed home from work for one day and would appreciate it if the merchandise could be delivered before nine in the morning or after five in the afternoon, or at some reasonably specific hour during the day. But often you won't be able to get such a promise. And while you have a right to be angry about that, you have to recognize that there are some things you can't change. Venting your emotions isn't going to get you what you want, and may just make matters worse.

However, if the problem you have called about once persists, the time has come to get tougher. That still doesn't mean yelling at anybody. It means getting through to someone higher up. That's not always easy. For one thing, the people at the lowest level don't like to pass problems on to their superiors because it makes it look as though they can't handle the job themselves. There's one technique that usually works, however.

Once again, you begin with your "good morning." Then you say, "I'm afraid you're talking to a very angry customer. I've tried to get this matter settled before through regular channels without success, and I think it would save everyone time if you put me through to your supervisor."

By *stating* that you're angry instead of actively *expressing* your irritation, you can get your point across without being nasty about it. Whoever you're talking to would probably just as soon avoid dealing with someone who's very angry. Since you haven't stated your problem, the representative has an out in terms of passing you along to a superior. He or she can say, "I've got a customer who says he's very angry. I don't know what the problem is, but apparently it's not a new one. He asked to talk to a supervisor. Will you take it?"

What's more, the supervisor comes on the line knowing that some care had better be taken, and is likely to start off by being solicitous—a fact that will help you to keep your emotions under control. At this point, the nicer you can manage to be the better. Expecting screams, the supervisor will be pleased to discover that, while upset, you are also rational and polite. That will increase rather than decrease your chances of getting action.

Niceness, in many cases, can get you everywhere.

Conclusion

You're going to your class reunion, your son's high school graduation, or attending a convention.

It's Thanksgiving or Christmas or Hanukkah, and there's going to be a big family reunion.

Your sister is getting married and there are going to be more than three hundred guests.

Your very rich Aunt Gertrude has died at ninety-three and the whole clan is attending the funeral.

You hope that the class reunion, the graduation, and the convention will be a lot of fun, that the holiday gathering will be joyous, that the wedding will be lovely, and the funeral sad but dignified.

Don't bet on it.

It seems as though every idiot you knew at college has turned up for the reunion. You and your wife are both attending your son's graduation; unfortunately, you were divorced just over a year ago and still aren't speaking. That holiday celebration is the perfect occasion for your mother and her sister-in-law to renew their long-standing feud. Your parents sharply disapprove of the fact that your sister is marrying a much older man. And as for your Aunt Gertrude, everyone in the family loathed the old skinflint.

Ritual gatherings can be and often are the highly enjoyable, memorable, or moving occasions they are meant to be. But the wise person will always keep in mind that they can also turn out be severe tests of one's niceness. Ritual gatherings, by their very nature as rites of passage or celebrations of renewal, bring on a sharpened awareness of the passage of time and a heightening of the emotions.

That means that normally nice people can easily go to pieces, get into arguments, and make fools of themselves. Ritual occasions also provide the perfect circumstances for people who are in the habit of making trouble to exercise their ability to stir things up. The nice person should thus approach all ritual gatherings fully prepared to tell a few white lies in an effort to prevent trouble, prepared to take sides or come to the rescue if confrontations develop, and forearmed against the possibility of being saddled with an unfair responsibility.

When attending graduations, class reunions, conventions, and large weddings, you are inevitably going to be meeting a number of people for the first time. That means that you will almost certainly find yourself dealing, nicely of course, with a raving jerk or two. At class reunions and conventions you can be quite sure that someone you know is going to get drunk. Maybe even you, which means that you should be particularly on guard against putting your foot in your mouth.

At almost any ritual gathering, someone is going to ask you a question you don't want to answer about a matter you'd rather keep private. Holidays, graduations, and weddings mean shopping for presents, which may turn you into an angry consumer. There are houseguests and unexpected children to cope with. Money issues can pop up at any moment, even at funerals—indeed, especially at funerals if rich Aunt Gertrude's will is as eccentric as she was.

For a great many people—as much as half the population of the country—ritual occasions present a special problem that deserves some attention. If you are divorced, divorced and remarried, the spouse of someone who has been divorced, or the son or daughter of divorced parents, ritual gatherings can be a particular trial. As Joe's second wife, I have first-hand knowledge of some of the curious and troublesome situations that can confront people touched by divorce.

If you are someone's second wife or second husband and you accompany your spouse to an event like a class reunion, there are going to be people who wonder who the hell you are. They knew the first wife or husband, perhaps well, perhaps only slightly. And since you'll be running into a lot of people whom your spouse hasn't really kept up with over the years, there can be confusion that may lead to embarrassing moments.

For everybody's sake, I think it's important for the nice person to clarify matters right up front. I say, "I'm Pat Raposo, Joe's second wife." I also try to let the person I'm talking to know that we've got two kids of our own and that Joe's two sons by his first marriage also live with us. By getting the facts out, you're helping the other person keep his foot out of his mouth, and lessening the possibility of having to answer awkward or insensitive questions yourself. You really don't want to have to deal with remarks like, "It's funny, but I remember you as a brunette," or "Oh, I didn't realize you were with Joe Raposo." Get it straight from the start.

The graduation from high school or college of the son or daughter of divorced parents presents an even trickier situation. Several classmates of Joe Jr.'s have found themselves in the position of dealing with parents who refused to attend any commencement event together. That means the kid has to go to the school concert with his mother, the graduation dinner with his father, and suffer the embarrassment of arranging for them to be seated far apart for the graduation exercises. I don't think any nice person should do that to his or her kids. If you're really adamant about not getting within a hundred feet of your former spouse at a child's graduation, then you shouldn't go. Period. Because all you're going to achieve is to make your kid absolutely miserable.

On the other hand, no nice person should be in the business of telling a child that they can't or mustn't attend a ritual gathering that involves a divorced spouse. My friend Louise, who's in her early thirties, was informed by her mother that if she went to her father's wedding to his second wife, her mother would never speak to her again. Louise cared about both her parents, and her mother's attitude put her into an impossible bind. If she did go, her mother would be in a rage; if she didn't, her father would be deeply hurt. She was being asked to take sides when she didn't want to. In the end she decided that her mother was really trying to use her as an instrument to wound her father—and she couldn't allow that to happen. She went to the wedding, as she should have. When the nice person is pressured to take sides, he or she has every right to go against the wishes of the individual who's issuing threats. Louise's mother, by the way, stuck to her threat of not speaking to Louise for exactly two weeks.

While the ramifications of divorce may complicate matters for the nice person on ritual occasions, the guidelines that I've focused on in the course of this book continue to apply. A divorce in the family changes the context—just as a marriage, a birth, a serious illness, money problems or a death in the family change the context. We can't hope to respond appropriately, nicely, unless we maintain the flexibility to adapt our approach to a situation in light of its particular nature. And as we define the context for ourselves, we need to keep in mind the three main responsibilities of the nice person discussed at the beginning of this book: the responsibility to avoid hurting or embarrassing other people unnecessarily, the responsibility to prevent bad situations from getting worse, and the responsibility to be true to our own standards.

In order to avoid hurting people, we need to avoid the temptation, in many situations, to be totally honest; whether we are turning down an invitation, responding to someone's request that we say "what we really think," or trying to avoid being imposed on, a few well-tuned white lies will serve us far better than absolute frankness. Yet there are other times when we have to lay it on the line in order to be true to our own standards. In crisis situations, such as when we come to the rescue of someone seriously in need of help, it may be necessary to be very blunt. In determining the difference between circumstances that call for a white lie and those that are better served by a degree of bluntness, we need to ask ourselves which approach is going to achieve the result we want with the least friction. If we really feel it's time to lay it on the line we have to be prepared to accept the consequences of our actions, and be sure that we're really helping and not just interfering.

We have to keep in mind at all times that it's a very small world, and make certain we know who our audience is before we launch into careless expressions of our opinions, especially if they happen to be negative. If we don't know our audience, we're bound to keep putting our feet in our mouths, causing other people distress, and embarrassing ourselves. On the other side of the coin, as nice people we need to recognize when it is important to take sides or stand up for our friends, at the same time trying to do so in ways that avoid out-and-out confrontation. Even when we conclude that our major responsibility is to ourselves, we should attempt to deal with things in a manner that fulfills the objective of making the situation better, not worse.

In the course of this book, we've looked at how to avoid being imposed upon, how to get out of unfair responsibilities, and how to deflect prying or rude questions about matters we'd rather keep private. In all of these areas, it's the good defense that wins the game; you don't have to become offensive yourself when dealing with offensive people.

The general guidelines I've presented here are adaptable to a great variety of circumstances. We've seen how to cope with raving jerks, drunks, clinging-vine houseguests, people who want to bring their children to adult parties, cheapskates, and the money-obsessed among us. As I said at the start, this book is not intended to be an encyclopedia, and the illustrative anecdotes I've used are based on my own experience. There are many situations you may find yourself in that aren't specifically dealt with here. But if you remember to examine the context before reacting, taking into account the who, what, where, and why of things, and think clearly about the responsibilities you have to other people and yourself, I believe that you can be a really nice person in almost any situation. Make use of the guidelines, and do it your way.

In a changed and changing world, hard-and-fast rules often don't apply. Being a nice person means being a flexible person. Indeed, being nice is finally another way of growing as a human being.

Index

Index